The Globe Toddler

Stefanie Schmitz

Published by
Sandy Roads Books
707 Sabur Ct., Cape Coral, FL 33904

Printed and bound in the United States of America

Cover Design © Mathew Riedl
Photographs © Stefanie Schmitz

ISBN 0-9773101-0-8

www. stefanieschmitz.com

For obvious reasons certain names in this book have been changed.

To my children Miles and Luna

Contents

Acknowledgements

Many people deserve thanks from me. I trust that they know who they are. I very much appreciate their support and encouragement. Special thanks go to my husband Michael Korzeniewski, my editor Andrew Randall, Stefan Kühlem, Mathew Riedl, Amanda Harris, Sylvia Neumann and Elisabeth Davies.

Preface

There are only two lasting bequests we can hope
to give our children.
One of these is roots, the other, wings.
- Hodding Carter

I was the last passenger to climb into the dark, hot bus. Taxi drivers had cornered me on the crowded parking area of the bus station. With their wild gestures and urgent looks they had tried to convince me that my bus had already left. Bastards! I didn't believe them. Resorting to my grimmest facial expressions for help I fought my way through to the ticket office. It was difficult, with a 50-pound heavy backpack and a two-year-old boy.

Everything in life happens for a reason, my best friend used to say. All seats were taken. The conductor pointed to the front.

I shook my head, mumbling, 'No, sir, I am not driving.'

He paused to digest my silly remark then he grabbed Miles by his hand and led him to our seat next to the bus driver. Yes, we had plenty of legroom.

I had bought only one ticket, which meant child on lap. But with the space we had Miles could sit on the floor if he wanted to. We had no seatbelts. Of course not. Where do you think we were? We sat shut off from the rest of the bus, which was overloaded with East Africans, their pets and their belongings. As soon as we left Arusha, our stuffy cockpit became the stage set for loud conversations in Swahili between the conductor and the driver.

At each stop, papers with lists of passengers passed back and forth. And packages passed through the window, barely missing our heads. The conductor got off to police the departure and arrival of people, then he jumped back on the bus, which was already in motion, and squeezed between the driver and us. He entertained the driver nonstop with what I gathered must have been gossip that he picked up along the route. Our bus fulfilled several functions: It was the North Tanzanian people transport, the postal delivery service and the mobile news exchange.

After what must have been five or six hours we finally stopped to take a break. I hurried to buy a fresh supply of cool drinks and to perform a diaper change. Miles lay on the concrete floor of the rough-looking ladies' restroom. Never mind the germs. I looked around for the sink to wash our hands, but I didn't see anything of that sort.

Back in the bus, Miles's fine blond hair curled from the sweat and stuck to my arm. He stretched himself and kicked back on my lap. Content, he munched his humid, rubber-like cookies, observed the bus driver and gurgled at every joke that this charming, middle-aged individual told in Swahili, while my legs fell asleep.

The villages that we passed were no larger than a handful of houses scattered along the roadside, but they were vibrant with life. A guy from Botswana, who I had met in Arusha, told me that during the time of president Julius Nyerere the Tanzanian population was encouraged to move from the back country to the main roads so that it was easier to supply them with electricity and water.

Then the bus stopped. Two people got off. Crowds of children surrounded the vehicle. Their skinny, long arms stretched toward the sky like Gospel singers stretching toward the heavens. Desperately pleading, they held in their hands whatever they had for sale: Peeled oranges, peanuts in long, see-through plastic bags, and old-style Coca-Cola bottles neatly stacked in wooden boxes. I saw a chicken dash in front of a motorcyclist. Feathers flew in the air. The chicken barely made it. Women greeted us with big smiles and waving hands.

The road in-between the villages was tiringly straight. The agricultural environment on both sides of the highway hardly changed.

'Mama, luuuk.' The slender, good-humored African bus driver pointed to the horizon.

His face beaming with a broad smile, his head nodded.

'Oh, please, not again,' I thought.

A vehicle had appeared in front of us, still a tiny spot in the far distance. The bus driver was the first one to see it. He honked the horn once in acknowledgement, then twice as the vehicle came closer, because he couldn't bear the tension. He honked three times to signal to the driver, 'My big fat bus is right behind you. I am actually close enough to hit you.' He overtook and honked four times in triumph. His African enthusiasm was excusable, I thought his night-clubish honking, not. Every honk set off a series of green, red, yellow and orange traffic lights, which had been installed one above the other on the right hand side of the front window. To Miles's delight these lights flickered fast and bright, each time in a different sequence, producing an equally different sequence of deafening *humptata* sounds. His toddler hands flew up in the air and he screeched with amusement.

I sign-languaged to the driver my approval, although his honking ritual annoyed the hell out of me, especially as I was just about to doze off. Yet I was relieved to see that my son was enjoying himself. The 12-hour bus ride from Arusha to Dar es Salaam, the capital city of Tanzania, was bearable for him. It could have been so different. I had taken a great chance.

Eventually, we arrived in the capital and I got out of the bus as fast as I could with my toddler under one arm and my bag under the other. I pushed us to the front of the line of people who surrounded the luggage that was being torn out from underneath the bus and dumped on the ground in one huge pile. I grabbed my backpack before somebody else decided to take a liking to it. Then I noticed that in my haste we had left Miles's comic book on the bus.

Without this comic book there was no further travel possible, not for me, not for Miles. My little one was able to immerse himself an incredible 30 minutes at a time into the picture stories. The book has about 40 pages, filled with adventure stories about this team of six goofy characters who outwit anything nasty that crosses their way simply because of the high quality leather shoes that they wear. You can't buy the book in a bookstore, it is published by a shoe store in Germany, hence the content.

The bus driver came running after us waving the shoe book. I ripped it out of his hands and shouted, 'Asante sana', thank you in Swahili.

We jumped into a taxi and Miles crawled on my lap. It was still warm. Car seats for children are a rarity in most places on this planet.

Barely at our destination, but before I had all the luggage and the fare sorted with the taxi driver, Miles had already disappeared. You have to be incredibly fast as a mother, unless you keep your toddler on a leash. But there comes a point when you are so tired and worn out that you can't chase anymore. I was in low gear. As I dragged my feet and our luggage through the entrance door, this was what I saw: Three Swedish tourists, two English backpackers, the Indian hotel owner and his wife laughing and staring at Miles. He already held the room key in his hands. He ran in circles, let himself fall on the ground, stood up, ran in a zigzag, attempted to hop on one leg, all the while performing verbal somersaults. And what was I – the mother - doing?

Legs stiff, stomach empty, I fell on the red vinyl sofa next to the other tourists.

'Where had we come from?' the Swedes wanted to know. 'From Arusha? By bus? No way!'

For a moment I didn't believe it myself.

Miles was uncomplaining, tranquil, almost stoic during this mammoth trip. Perhaps you suspect that I put a few drops of whiskey in his milk. Or perhaps I am the lucky mother of an extraordinary child. Neither of which is true, of course. The only meaningful explanation that I can find is what a friend of mine once said to me: The most important thing is that parents are happy and content with what they do. It reflects on the child.

And when it comes to riding the bus in a foreign country, I believe you will have a hard time finding anyone who is more passionate about it than me. I feel more in contact with people and I see more. It's as natural to me as to the many families in Africa that rely on public transport. I lean back and relax while the country pops up on the horizon like on a movie screen. And I don't worry about anything, not even about the madly driving chauffeur who, while I am looking out of the window, has to deal with bad roads, an ancient bus and a male ego.

Besides the comic book and some snacks, I never brought anything else for Miles in my carry-on luggage. I needed the remaining space for tickets, some small change, a map maybe. Surprisingly, it never mattered. The human expects what he is used to. Children and adults are the same. Or rather children have even fewer preconceived ideas about how things should be. Therefore, the earlier we travel with our kids the easier they adapt.

I thoroughly enjoy backpacking, sometimes off the beaten track, sometimes not, in strange and foreign lands. For most people low-budget backpacking would be their worst nightmare, let alone with a young child in tow. I imagine that parents lack the confidence to travel with young children far away from their comfortable and secure homes in the Western World because they have no previous travel experience. People need to understand that contrary to popular belief, our technologically and industrially advanced world isn't necessarily safe than any other place on this planet. And what would actually happen if we were to look beyond the borders of our own country? Well, there are countries out there with so much wildlife they are zoos without bars, and with so many attractions and activities they are Disney World without the crowds.

I had been a solo traveler for ten years when Miles came into my life. My adventuring began with a low budget trip to Jamaica. I was a naïve young woman then, on her own, with a return ticket from London to Kingston. It was only when the taxi hastened through the dark streets of Trenchtown and I saw piles of garbage and armed people everywhere that I realized what I had gotten myself into. The taxi stopped abruptly in front of the modest guesthouse that I had chosen out of the pitiful travel guide. As I stepped out of the car a young Jamaican, who introduced himself as my best friend on the island, greeted me. He offered to sell me something to smoke. I declined politely. When I left the guesthouse the next morning my best friend was already waiting for me. Although I chose to ignore him he followed me like a fly. I flagged down a local bus at random and got on. It worked. I got rid of the Rasta, however, I had no idea where I was going.

For the next three weeks persistent Jamaican men followed me and talked my ear off. A typical one-sided conversation sounded like this:

'Have you ever had a black man in bed? ... Would you like to try one? ... We could smoke together? ... I have some *guuud* ganja, man.'

But despite the bother and the gruesome stories that fellow male backpackers told about robberies and stabbings, I survived. Not only that, I couldn't wait to go on my next trip, equipped with a flight ticket, a useful guidebook this time, and a backpack.

There are two people living in my soul: the daring one and the one that fears and worries. The nervous one always takes over, the day before departure. I can tell because I rummage round my bedroom restlessly not knowing what to pack, and I often wonder: Why do I put myself through this? Only to prove that I can overcome my fears, the limits that were instilled in me during my childhood? Yes, but there is more than that.

As soon as I set foot on new ground my mind and my soul feel free and independent. Traveling creates an enormous breathing space inside me that sharply contrasts with my life, whose daily routines and duties I perceive as stifling. I shook off the many untrue and unnecessary preconceptions that I had been taught about other countries. Repeatedly I made the experience that it is us, the Westerners, who are afraid, who need a predictable life and insurances, and not the ones who live under poorer conditions. Eventually, foreign grounds became my home - to such an extent that my home became foreign. A sobering lesson.

I was 30 years old and a changed person when I returned to Europe after three years in Costa Rica. I was also seven months pregnant with Miles. Since I had seen no different in Costa Rica, I believed that I could get away with rushing to the nearest hospital once contractions started without making prior arrangements. I believed that I could do without a pram. I

planned to tie my newborn on my back and nurse him
wherever I was, in the shop, in the subway or in the restaurant.
My gynecologist stared at my in disbelief when I pulled out a
3x3-inch card with my blood group and a few check-up dates
in it.

'That's all you have?' he asked.

'Yes,' I said.

His mouth wouldn't close. I stared back at him. I didn't
know what else to say. When he recovered from his shock he
made me undergo hundreds of tests. But he wasn't the only
one who believed I needed help. Young mothers who lived in
the neighborhood pulled me in and out of baby stores. Their
shopping lists grew longer and longer and my eyes got bigger
and bigger. I was astounded by the array of products that
swing, rotate, lift and speak to your baby. They even sold baby
phones. Now, babies can't speak, so what on earth do they
need these things for?

I was confused and insecure, ignorant, if you will. In Costa
Rica I had seen a different picture of how to raise children. A
less complicated, but more natural one, so it seemed to me.
And it was this particular picture that ultimately formed my
ideas about traveling with Miles.

When he was born I was a single parent. My family and
friends gently reminded me that I ought to be responsible –
now that I was a mother. In other words, get your act together
and discontinue living like a gypsy! But I believed that Miles
would be an asset to my previously lonesome globetrotting and
that traveling would be an asset to his development. I just
needed to prove it to them, and a little bit to myself, too.

Miles and I moved to England, where we settled down and
lived life in conformity with society's norms. Nevertheless, I

went ahead and introduced Miles to traveling as early as possible. In the frequent school holidays that I enjoyed as a teacher I took baby Miles on trips to Northern Spain, Ghana, Southern France and Cyprus.

After two years of teaching, remodeling a house, entertaining lazy au pairs and trying to be the perfect mom, I noticed that not only had I quite naturally failed at being perfect, but also that my hair was slowly turning gray. I longed to spend some bonding time with my toddler son. I owed it to him. Surely he was fed up with seeing his mother only on evenings and at weekends. And more fed up with shopping in decorating stores and watching mom bang nails, saw wood and paint. The need to create a breathing space in our lives and to get a new perspective on what our relationship is all about became apparent. The idea developed to travel to Africa and to try to survive out there for as long as two month's salary would permit. I gave up my job, rented my house to colleagues and set off to visit friends in Nairobi and near Embu, Central Kenya. After that, Miles and I went on a camping trip to Tanzania. Five months later we returned to Europe.

In Africa I met him, the fearless Alaskan, my future husband and soul mate, but only briefly. Little did I know back then that two years after our first encounter Mike would invite us to Alaska and propose to me on the summit of Pioneer Peak. By then I had signed a one-year teaching contract at a school in Spain, and that's where we headed next. From there Miles, Mike and I took off on a six-month long 'Tour de World'. Miles was four years old.

On our way around the globe, fellow travelers of all ages inundated us with their questions: 'How do you do it?' 'What does your child eat and drink?' 'What about the diseases he

could catch?' 'Is it a hassle for you?' 'Aren't you afraid?'
Followed by exclamations such as: 'What a lucky boy he is.' 'I
wish my parents had taken me around the world when I was
four.'

I soaked up their fascination and secret admiration like a dry
sponge, because, after all, my own people at home had only
criticized me for what I exposed Miles to. The two arguments
that I heard the most were that I seemed oblivious to the
dangers that mortal viruses, low standards of hygiene and child
abduction could pose to the life of my son; and that young
children need to grow up with routines.

In retrospect I confess I only pretended not to be aware of
the dangers of traveling outside of Europe and the United
States. They even tormented me at times. But I didn't let them
become blown out of proportion and I applied what I had
learned on previous trips.

Also, traveling isn't intrinsically without routine. I managed
to put Miles to bed at the same time every day with very few
exceptions. Whether we were in a plane, a camper or having to
pitch up our tent, bedtime was at 7 o'clock. We established
beach routines, shower routines and story time routines. Not
enough to convince everybody. For some I remain an
irresponsible, or more politely phrased, incomprehensible
mother.

Let's look at the bright side. There is so much to gain for
children. I longed to equip Miles with the wings of linguistic
ability, cultural tolerance, acceptance of diversity, and a hands-
on knowledge about other people and their ways of living. We
live in a century in which more than ever before we need
young people to acquire a global vision.

Of course, traveling with a toddler is different from traveling without one, but so is life. It takes extra effort to travel with a child, but by the same token, traveling becomes much more enriching. I have slowed down my travel pace to a healthier one. I have met more people and visited fewer museums. And I have experienced motherhood as a universal link between women of all races and cultures, which in turn has granted me a unique access to other societies. I have witnessed how a little person explores the world without prejudice, and how he adapts with mysterious ease. Miles has taught me flexibility and patience, and heightened my tolerance for dirty toilets. Our voyages have been an unforgettable bonding time between a mom and a son.

Many countries around the globe have served my family as both playground and classroom. Traveling was scary on certain days - when we thought that we had made mistakes, when our egos got in the way, and when we didn't pass the tests that we set ourselves - but on most days traveling was rewarding. We learned new things and made new friends, and played hard.

I didn't travel with Miles with the intention to write a book about it, but neither did I expect that traveling with children to countries beyond the Western World would still be such a hot issue. My book is a contribution to this debate, not a 'How to' travel guide. I am not one to give advice, just encouragement, because traveling with the purpose of educating yourself and your children as world citizens is worth all the effort and risks it involves.

August 2005

1

Ghana

Backpacking with Baby Bottles

It was pitch dark outside. I turned to the taxi driver and asked the obvious: 'Is there no electricity?'

'No, Ma'am,' he responded politely and laughed. 'It's been like this for a while. You see, the rainy season is nearly over but we haven't had much rain. The water level in the Volta River is very low. Is this your first time in Ghana?'

'No,' I lied.

'Well, then, you know that here in Accra we get all our electricity from the huge Akosombo Dam at the Volta Lake.

When the water levels are low our government shuts the power off. Rationing, they call it, or something like that.'

He laughed again, as if he had told us a joke. Never on earth would he have understood my insignificant worries, and I decided not to talk. Instead I thought to myself, 'What will Miles eat and drink tonight and all day tomorrow? I need electricity to boil the water for the instant milk formula and to warm his food. I wish I could still nurse him. Accra without electricity. Why am I not prepared for this kind of scenario? I wished we had gone to Italy.'

Ever since I have had the pleasure of meeting African students at the universities of Wales, Leeds and Bristol I have felt intrigued by the tales they had to tell and fascinated by their cultures, so different from ours. I listened to stories about voodoo, survival, religion, ceremonies and the new democracies. According to my Mali friend, democracy is a form of governance that allows people to cross the street when the traffic lights are still red. I admired the way they coped with tragedies. They never complained, and always held their heads up high. I wanted to see Africa with my own eyes.

When time and money allowed me to go on my first Africa trip I happened to be the mother of a one-year-old baby who was still crawling over the polyester carpet. It didn't bother me as much as it seemed to bother everyone else who wasn't going.

Where exactly in Africa I would visit I decided on one of those lousy, rainy, mind-numbingly boring weekends in February. I threw a dart at the map and it landed on Ghana. Ghana, Benin, Togo, Senegal, Ivory Coast, ... which one of the slices of the West African cake is which? They all look the same, geographically speaking. But in real terms the differences are enormous. Which ones are travel safe? And where do people speak English? I refused to travel to the former French colonies, since my school French would have limited me to buying *croissants* and *l'eau minérale*. The more I read about Ghana, however, the more I believed that it was the perfect destination for an Africa greenhorn like me. Politically and economically stable, small, not too spoiled by tourism, but still truly African.

I thought hard if I knew of anyone who had been to Ghana. Fortunately, not a soul came to my mind, and that made me feel like a pioneer. Most people probably don't even know where Ghana is. I searched my brain for what I knew about Ghana and two names sprung to my mind - Kofi Annan, the United Nations Secretary-General, and Kwame Nkrumah, the former president who, in 1957, led what was then the Gold Coast from British rule to independence. It was the first black African country to leave colonialism behind.

Reading more about my holiday destination I learned that the ancient Empire of Ghana was celebrated for its wealth of gold, hence its former name. In the seventeenth and eighteenth centuries the Gold Coast contributed about 10,000 slaves each year to the Atlantic slave trade. Ghana's coast is dotted with forts and castles that are monuments to that trade.

Despite Ghana's economic recovery in recent decades it is still one of the poorest countries in the world. So what was I really going to do over there except quench my thirst for adventure and African culture? Was I going to hike through whatever is left of Ghana's tropical rainforests on the lookout for leopards and elephants, accidentally stepping on a cobra with Miles on my back? I didn't think so. A beach holiday customized for one-year-olds would be a much better choice. And Ghana has just that: More than 300 miles of sandy, uncrowded coastline were luring us for some serious playtime.

One thing about guidebooks is that they never tell you the truth. They describe the countries in the rosiest colors they can get away with. 'Accra is the most vibrant capital in West Africa, where mid-range hotels with air conditioning and restaurants offer Western standard choices for travelers,' it reads. Accra appeared in front of my eyes as the African twin sister of Panama City. I was going to be disappointed. Guidebooks are also notorious for exaggerating dangers. As a world traveler you become immune to these overcautious warnings. The probability that a car will hit you on a highway in your own country is much higher than becoming the victim of some foreign criminals on your next holiday, no matter where you go. The warnings about Ghana said that mugging and harassment of women especially around hotels, is frequently reported. With the exception of Morrisville, New York, this is probably true for any town or city in the world. I wasn't afraid. Who would be so heartless as to mug a mother with a baby? Muggers go for affluent looking tourists with cameras and golden wristwatches, not moms with babies. So, there you have it. Traveling with small children has its advantages. Miles's presence made him and me, his guardian angel, untouchable, even if only in my imagination. It had the effect that in the company of my one-year-old I was more courageous and daring than when I had traveled alone. A contradiction in itself that really isn't one.

In any case violent human behavior seems more predictable at least, when compared with vicious attacks of malaria transmitting anopheles mosquitoes, tsetse flies, tumba flies or, even weirder, worms that can grow up to several hundred inches long inside your body and have to be extracted out of your behind over a period of several weeks. Not to mention the intolerable number of invisible bacteria West Africa is littered with. Hence, both my arms succumbed to a myriad of painful needles: Hepatitis A, typhoid, diphtheria, yellow fever … The short, chubby English nurse at the neighborhood health clinic took vivid interest in our visits. She had never opened so many of her white rollout drawers, each a buffet filled with pharmaceutical delicatessen. Not surprising, given that she worked in a part of town where the average patient would consider the two-hour train ride to London an adventure.

'All right,' she said, looking at my swollen arm. 'You need to come back for your hepatitis A booster, Miles for his yellow fever, and then we are done.'

As I walked to my car that afternoon I felt so boosted I was convinced that I would never fall sick again for the rest of my life. I was convinced that my body would reject any virus and any vitamin there was. But the hepatitis A booster was neither the last chemical nor the worst to enter my body. I had to start taking anti-malarial drugs.

Malaria is a dangerous disease that must be taken seriously by any traveler who visits the tropics. It kills about 2 million people worldwide each year and the number is increasing. Unfortunately, a strain of malaria resistant to chloroquine – one of the milder preventative drugs - is prevalent throughout

West Africa. Larium, the most effective and commonly prescribed drug, comes with a list of side effects that makes you wonder if it wouldn't be more fun to contract malaria. Anecdotal evidence suggests that the anti-malarial drug can cause almost everything you can think of, from simple headaches and nausea to hallucinations, depression and sleep disturbances. I even knew of a real life example, a young guy from San Francisco, who threw his coat and rucksack down the mountain of Kilimanjaro. He said his heart was racing and he felt an unexplainable joy as he watched his belongings roll down. The otherwise completely sane guy blamed the Larium tablet that he had taken that morning for his psychotic outbreak. So, the choices that I had to protect us from malaria looked grim. I could have stayed home of course, but my flight tickets were bought, so I had to think of something else. I couldn't get myself to swallow Larium, so I went halfway instead. I took chloroquine and I wore long-sleeved shirts, long pants and socks (I hate wearing socks) in the evenings. Then I made up my mind about Miles. He was too young to take any anti-malarial. I planned to protect him well enough so that he wouldn't get stung in the first place. Zero mosquito bites and he can't get malaria. It is a feasible option when you are traveling for only a short period of time.

I purchased a special type of pre-treated mosquito net. It kills mosquitoes as soon as they sit on it, that way Miles would be safe when he slept. The malaria virus-carrying female anopheles mosquito is a nighttime feeding insect that takes its meal of blood from the unsuspecting victim in the cool hours of dusk and dawn. Miles never woke up before it was light outside and that's when the mosquito had stopped her activities for the day. When she returned to her mission around

6 p.m. Miles would lie well tucked under his net listening to a goodnight story. Problem solved.

Two weeks before we left I counted diapers with the same nervous accuracy a smoker counts the last cigarettes for the night. I was pretty sure that I wouldn't find diapers in Ghana's coastal villages amongst fresh fish and *fufu*, an African porridge. At the end of the day, baby formula, a miniature kettle for boiling water, two baby bottles, some clothes for Miles, Pampers, a hat, sunscreen with a protection factor of 150, and a Dr. Seuss book about 'feet' filled over three-quarters of my backpack. Just a few inches were left for my own stuff, three outfits. The only thing that could possibly go wrong and mess up my meticulously planned I-am-totally-in-control vacation was if 16-months-old Miles would pooh a few times too many. Then we would run out of diapers, a stressful experience for any first-time mother, but hopefully not the end of the world. Miles blew out his cheeks and pulled himself upright, both hands clutching the strings of the backpack. He was ready to go and do some exploring. Just a few days ago he had tried to put one foot in front of the other without losing balance. I guess he didn't care where on this planet he was going to continue his walking practice, on the living room carpet in our Bristol home or on the grass in front of an African hotel. Both offer comparative softness.

The telephone rang. It was my friend Sylvia from Hamburg. Somehow she had heard about our trip and contemplated joining us. There was just one problem: Miles. Never in her life would she have envisaged traveling with a child, let alone a baby. She was afraid that the potentially rewarding adventure would turn into a trip from hell because Miles wouldn't be able to cope.

'I would love to go, but I'm not quite sure if I want to do this with Miles,' she said honestly. 'Does he sleep through the night?'

'Yes. Twelve hours nonstop,' I replied.

'Does this mean he never wakes up? Even when he has a bad dream?'

'No. Never.' It was true.

'So, we could go down to the hotel bar at night and have a drink without Miles?'

'Yes, of course,' I laughed. 'We just need to check on him every so often.'

'Does he whine a lot?'

'Only when he is thirsty or bored.'

'What are we going to do with him when we want to go places and do sightseeing?'

'I will carry him on my back in the baby carrier.'

Okay. She would come, she said. I was excited, and I didn't care which of us two had passed the interview, Miles the super sleeper, or I, with my laissez-faire attitude? Ultimately, I think it was the exotic destination that made the whole deal so tempting for a passionate traveler like her. When would she ever find anyone to go to Ghana with?

Shortly before our departure she called once more. She told me that her colleagues had displayed great skepticism when they heard that she was going to go on a trip to West Africa with a child.

'They think I have lost it,' she reported. 'And the things they said about you, I don't even dare to repeat.'

She didn't need to. I knew what they had said and I was used to it by now.

My little one and I flew from London to Amsterdam. One hour later Sylvia arrived from Hamburg. We met her at the gate. Our connecting flight to Accra would leave in seven hours. The wait could have turned into seven dreadful hours had Miles been unable to sleep. Therefore, we were more than happy when we discovered that Amsterdam Airport has a baby room with beds and changing tables and dim lighting. It's a quiet, announcement-free zone.

I felt like changing into my pajamas and going to sleep. I was envious. Anyway, I changed Miles into a pair of comfy pajamas and put him to bed. Immediately, he stood up and looked around. 'Oh,' I thought, 'perhaps he is not going to sleep with all this action around him.' But he watched the other children going to bed and this must have changed his mind. He waved goodnight to everybody and I laid him down. It was so much more fun to go to bed in the company of others.

Hovering over our Ghana books in the semi-dark room and whispering to each other, Sylvia and I roughly planned out our vacation and chose the hotel we would stay in once we got to Accra.

Onboard the Dutch airline, the African adult passengers displayed a great tolerance for the lively children passengers, and the flight attendants bent all rules of safety and etiquette accordingly. Six-year-olds were allowed to serve water. They enjoyed running up and down the aisles, asking everyone a hundred times if they needed more.

Miles sat on the floor. For most of the trip he played with a toy car that we had bought at the airport. Every so often the car would shoot out into the aisle in front of someone's feet. Nobody complained. Nobody was bothered about all this confusion. Was this what Africa was going to be like? The atmosphere was relaxed, reassuring for my tense and wired self. I leaned back and saw Ghana coming up in front of my eyes. Finally I started to feel something like anticipation. I had nearly forgotten that I was supposed to look forward to the trip.

Humid heat pressed itself upon us. We were drenched just standing in line in the customs hall. Everything around us smelled sweaty and moist. I feared the worst from customs officials. I had been warned by my Nigerian friends about the bribery that is considered normal in West Africa. Prepared for the men in uniform to order me to open my backpack and poke their noses through my stuff, I smiled appeasingly. Nobody said a word to me. They hardly looked at me. Apparently, the Ghanaian officers aren't trying to keep up with their Nigerian counterparts, and tourists feel welcomed when they arrive rather than being robbed of half their spending money on their first day.

It was around ten at night when we left Accra International Airport, a barren building. Immediately, a shadowless darkness swallowed us. Just the white insides of large hands interrupted this darkness like the flicker of flashlights.

Miles was fast asleep in his stroller. Within seconds after landing he had passed out from the tropical heat. Now his head rested on his left shoulder, his arms hung loose like boiled spaghetti. I stood behind him. My backpack with a baby carrier hanging from it was taking up room for three. I was definitely taking up too much space in the tight crowd of people in the parking lot.

I had a quick nervous look around and couldn't fail to notice that we were the only white tourists. Everybody seemed to know exactly where they were going. I was the only one who stood around motionless like a frozen fish, waiting for Sylvia. She had gone to withdraw a thick bundle of Ghanaian cedi. Her extra pairs of hands and feet were already serving themselves as quite helpful, while my hands remained clutched to the handles of the stroller. I felt tired and wished I could just sit in Miles's place and sleep. Sleep. Not having to worry about the herd of taxi drivers that had discovered me as easy bait and was slowly encircling me. Taxi drivers are the worst at airports. They know you haven't got a clue about distances and prices and currencies. They are there to rip you off as much as they possibly can. As soon as Sylvia appeared the taxi drivers jumped on her. Since I hadn't shown any reaction to their theatrical performances, it must have made them assume I was deaf and dumb. Sylvia pretended that she knew Accra like the back of her hand. She rattled off a list of memorized hotel names. One of the hotels had just recently burned to the ground, we learned. Oh, shit! The other hotel names didn't ring anyone's bells. Our faces, our perplexed looks, Sylvia's talk, everything revealed the same truth: This was our first time in Ghana.

I took my guidebook out of the side pocket of my backpack. The taxi drivers all spoke at the same time with heavy accents. Then, all of a sudden, the rolling thunder of language came to a halt.

'Bellview Hotel,' I said, and looked up.

Too late. Our luggage had already disappeared in different directions. About five or six taxi drivers were eager to drive us to the place.

'Hold on,' I yelled. 'Stop! We only need ONE taxi.'

I yanked my backpack out of the trunk of the car closest to me and tried to shoulder my way through to my friend. Then I heaved Miles out of his stroller and the taxi driver squashed the stroller in-between the backpacks. Quite amazing how your luggage always fits in the trunk, isn't it? It doesn't seem to matter if you are traveling with one small bag or four oversize bags and two suitcases.

I fell on the plastic covered backseats of the beat-up taxi. Miles was opening his big brown eyes and he peered around startled, trying to make sense of the unfamiliar world. He tried to stand up on my lap, but his wobbly knees wouldn't keep him upright. We were swerving through the pitch black, paved arteries and unpaved, potholed veins of Accra.

Initially, the extreme darkness of my surroundings didn't make me wonder. A sudden halt, we shot forward. Miles rolled up like a pickled herring. The taxi driver maneuvered his car, a vehicle without the slightest hint of suspension, over a road horrendously cut up after months of no rain. We exchanged the smooth asphalt for dust with even more potholes and no pavements. I had memorized the downtown Accra map as best as I could and immediately recognized the street name as we entered the track to our hotel. That was when it occurred to me that the only lights we saw were the flickering flames of the charcoal fires to our right and left. The glooming orange faces that looked so alive and chatty belonged to the street vendors guarding their wooden carts and small barbecues. If I weren't so sure that I was in Africa I would have thought it was early Halloween. Sweets and meat kebabs on burnt sticks looked like the choice for our late night dinner. The people displayed a great patience with the ongoing situation. Not me. My body was in panic, or was it just a silly helplessness? No electricity!

More than 4,000 miles separated me from relatives and friends. Why did their preoccupations still bother me?

'In Africa children die like flies from eating and drinking contaminated food. Do you want Miles to catch parasites?' I conversed with myself. 'Of course, not.'

Barely two hours after arrival and I already regretted my love for adventurous trips. Deep in thought I carried our luggage piece by piece from the dusty, red street into the foyer. Miles sat patiently on one of the sofas. Sylvia darted across the street to get at least some bottled water for us, although the sealed bottle that sat in contaminated water to stay cool might not be the ideal solution. However, I didn't want to get into that now. My main concern was that Miles probably wouldn't drink the water, but would have a screaming fit instead which, in turn, would dehydrate him more than he already was.

Half-heartedly I checked us in, when all of a sudden the buzz of a diesel engine woke me up from this bad dream. Never before in my life had the annoying noise of a generator sounded so soothing. In fact, in all the emotional hecticness it hadn't registered in my brain that a few lights were giving life to the hotel. I thanked God and the Bellview Hotel.

We entered a small dark room with one small window. Now, why would someone decorate the walls of a room, that in its architecture already resembled a prison cell, with brown paint and complement it with a dark green carpet? Miles didn't care. He crawled in circles on the unfriendly, worn out flooring. After all, he had some muscles to exercise after so many hours of being on the road. Due to the unusual heat he drank not only his milk, but, to my great astonishment, half a gallon of cold, bottled water. I tucked him under the light cotton sheets and exhausted from the humidity he passed into the coma of the innocent.

It was a beautiful evening. The inviting courtyard of the hotel was furnished with summery white garden chairs, round bistro tables and leafy trees that branched out in an umbrella-like fashion. The spicy smell of meat kebabs sneaked over the courtyard walls. We felt protected from too many of those first impressions that overwhelm the traveler who enters unfamiliar worlds. Yet our ears and noses witnessed some of the vibrancy of Accra street life at night. Cool, refreshing local beer appeased our hungry stomachs. We toasted the day, tropical Africa and the generator. Open, talkative Ghanaians joined us for a little while, giving us advice on what to see and do. From where we sat I could see our room's window. It was dark. No sounds of Miles.

'The baby is sleeping well,' whispered the voice of a hotel employee next to my ear, as if he were going to wake him up had he spoken in a normal voice like everyone else out here. He tiptoed away. These people are very gentle, I thought.

2

Boys and Girls, Kings and Princes

Don't ask me why, exactly, I thought it a good idea to take a stroller along to a country with no pavements, few paved roads, but plenty of potholes, mud and sand. I might as well have taken a wheelbarrow – except that wheelbarrows are more difficult to check-in at the airport. It was too late anyway. We had arrived in Ghana and I was stuck with it, unless I wanted to dump it in the streets and watch who would pick it up and what he would use it for. I didn't dump it. Imagine the looks I got in Accra, when two days after our arrival, I tried to push Miles from the hotel entrance to the street corner. The stroller's wheels got stuck in the soft road surface and started to turn in the most awkward directions. One wheel wanting to go left, the other one right. It was early in the morning, but the exercise made me sweat profusely. Everyone seemed to stare at us and worse, smile. I leaned on the handles with the entire weight of my body, my backpack and hand luggage. That way at least we moved forward, at the speed of two inches per minute, but we moved. I was embarrassed about my ignorance. I looked like a damn tourist only hoping to be a traveler.

West Africans travel differently. The babies are tied to their mother's back in a cloth. That way the moms have both hands free to carry more luggage and the babies enjoy a good view. They are also protected from the exhaust fumes that blasted straight into Miles' face, sitting so low.

Africans travel with mountains of luggage. Bursting bundles, bags and cardboard boxes neatly held together by string. Why so much luggage? Ask any African to open his suitcase and you will find mangoes and pineapples between clothes. But they are able to move fast with all those pieces of luggage since they rarely travel alone. The women each balance a bag on their heads, they carry two with their hands, and the baby. Like a caravan of camels they manage to move in tranquil rhythm for long stretches, not tired from the weighty burdens. They look gracious and proud, with straight backs and long necks. Not crunched and restricted like us.

Africans don't trust backpacks. Too many little pockets and zips and strings. Besides, backpacks are designed to be carried by the wrong part of the body. And in an emergency you couldn't quickly throw it off your back. The straps are, therefore, considered stifling, breath taking, and unpractical in the eyes of the locals.

During the one day that Sylvia and I spent in Accra we visited the Makola market. I sat Miles in the baby carrier that sat like a backpack on my back. I nearly looked African then. We strolled through Accra's largest market looking for fresh fruits and CDs with Ghanaian drumming music. With its hundreds of stalls and vendors that line the pavement the Makola market is one of the craziest places I have visited in my life. In the midst of swarming activity women passed us carrying sewing machines on their heads, while others carried rows of nail varnish that wrapped around Styrofoam cylinders. Everyone was selling something, improvising. A bunch of giant snails took us by surprise. Peeking down on us from the rim of a round plastic bowl that rocked on a woman's head, these big animals appeared to be inflated. Huge, slimy things, the shape of gherkins. I imagined the horrified stares, the air-gasping, wide-open mouths the snail lady would meet if she were magically removed to a Florida shopping mall. Here, in Ghana, at least people glared at me in a humane sort of way. They probably pitied me. Ghanaians smile when they pity you. That's the impression they left with me.

For most of the Ghana trip the stroller and I separated. I hid it in the corner of the hotel room until it was time to move to a different place. In Elmina, our first stop along the coast, we stayed in a low-key resort, in a bungalow that was small but luxurious for African standards. We had tiled floors, a private bathroom, electricity and a terrace with ocean view. We were the only guests. Every once in a while the restaurant was filled with Africans in suits and ties doing business over lunch.

From the resort to Elmina, the coastal fishing village, it was quite a walk. I carried Miles back and forth. We enjoyed the town and visited it several times during our stay. It is a town that lacks sanitary sewage. It is a town with only three modest looking restaurants. The houses reflect the simple lifestyle of their owners. Yes, it is one of those towns that looks like the majority of towns in this world: The population lives in mud huts or concrete walls with an aluminum roof, and they lack sufficient income to send their children to school.

Elmina's people are remarkably friendly, as Sylvia and I experienced one afternoon when we had set out to exchange some of our traveler's checks. We walked from bank to bank in the gloomy heat of the day. Believe it or not, nobody knew what to do with those things. The bank clerks turned them around, held them upside down and then handed them back to us with a smile. No, never seen before. Instead of getting a headache over the money we climbed Elmina's peninsula, curious to see its famous castle from the inside. The Portuguese built the castle in 1471. Whitewashed, it sits on a rocky hill overlooking the ocean and the small fishing community.

All of a sudden we heard a 'Hello, hello' echoing off the thick stone walls that surrounded us. Someone followed us with urgent steps. We turned around and saw a young man in a blue suit and tie, breathlessly pushing his bicycle. He spoke fast. He seemed to know us.

'I think he is one of those bank clerks that we spoke to about one hour ago,' Sylvia said.

I was startled. How did he find us? And why did he come running after us? He came with good news. A few miles out of town there was a hotel where we might be able to exchange our checks. It wasn't true, as we found out later, after we had walked those miles, but still, the dedication with which he tried to help us was flattering. And it revealed a lot about the nature of the people. Deprived of the typical amenities that we find in our hometowns, Elmina felt strangely pleasant, unspoiled and doubtlessly safe.

Whenever we go back in history we wonder about the brutality of the human. Here, in Elmina, the traveler meets the reminiscence of a place that served as the largest slave trading post in the world. Here slaves were tortured beyond anyone's imagination. A disturbing thought that lingered around when we walked over the cobbled stones. Today, Elmina's people live together harmoniously and safe from foreign intruders.

The town must have buried its memories of the slave traders deep. Our encounters with the local people were refreshingly free of any prejudice. I had expected a certain animosity towards us. Although, or perhaps because, we were the only fair-skinned visitors that the town had seen in a while, people were genuinely welcoming to us.

After eight days we left Elmina in the early morning hours before the heat of the day set in and I promised myself to come back one day to spend more time in this place.

I had already tormented the young clerk at the reception desk of our resort for some time. We needed some sort of transport to get to the official bus stop for the buses to Winneba. After all, it was a long way through a stretched-out village then further along the main road.

'I'm very sorry, my lady, but this early in the morning I cannot get a taxi for you. The hotel has a shuttle service. If you care to wait for about two hours, we will be delighted to bring you to the bus stop for only a small charge.'

The smart-looking receptionist was polite but rather unemotional, un-African. The pitiful paraphernalia that hung from my fragile shoulders and Miles's overloaded stroller didn't move him in the slightest.

'We will have to walk to the main street and flag down a taxi by ourselves.' Sylvia summed up my unsuccessful efforts.

Why was she always so annoyingly relaxed about everything? I could already hear my backbone crack and knew that it was going to be one of those painful situations that you stash away and hope to remember when you have grandchildren. Then I will think it was funny. Hence I didn't complain, but, hey, our little fellow did. His size two feet kicked impatiently against the front bar of the stroller as if to say, now that I'm tied into this thing, I want to get moving. Come on. Action. Push.

While we were crawling like turtles off the hotel grounds every member of the staff, besides the receptionist, came to say farewell to Miles. Not to us, of course, to Miles. They worshipped him. A last feel of his soft white arm, of his soft golden hair. A last word in English, a blessing in *Twi* or *Fanti*, and a last smile at his holy face were all-important.

Miles wasn't moved. It was far too early to be smiley and nice. He was looking along the narrow sandy path that wound its way through the tall coconut palm trees, resembling totem poles in the mist. When do we finally get some action going? Push faster, his eyes implored. But as soon as we left the asphalt of the hotel entrance my arms and hands started to shake. I felt the urge to swear and to kick the back of this sturdy pushchair, but I refrained. Instead I promised the world that upon my return from this trip I was going to invent a 4x4 stroller. One with huge wheels and a motor that makes it go over any kind of ground and through any kind of weather. It probably wouldn't pass regulations. What did I care?

Just a few steps into the hut village and my pointless brain exercises that diverted my anger became needless. Plenty of excited little helpers were running toward us. More children spotted us and abandoned their play in the shade in front of their thatched homes.

Word got round like a bushfire. Boys and girls skipped over to us in small groups, each group being led by the older brothers and sisters. Behind them the smaller ones stumbled along, trying to keep up. Children not older than 10 months moved their tiny bare feet incredibly fast to keep up, the tips of their T-shirts or dresses stuck in their mouths. Nervously they continued to chew on their clothes while their older, more confident siblings reached out to touch the 'magic thing', in other words: the stubborn, old stroller.

Most of the children talked loudly in *Ewe*. It sounded as if they were shouting orders. A few kept silent and stared curiously at Miles. The toddlers still chewed on their dresses. By the time we had passed the first five palm-thatched huts, the heads of mothers and fathers appeared in the doorless frames of their mud dwellings. Before long the entire village population, except for those who had already left for work, formed a guard of honor alongside the sandy path. The crowd of children around Miles and his rotten vehicle multiplied like a swarm of bees after the queen bee had settled. I hadn't realized that huts so few in number and so small in size could be the homes of so many people.

I was appeased, my anger blown away. Clearly, these Ghanaians had never in their lives seen a stroller, even though we are talking about what would be an outdated model in my country. The village grew animated and high-pitched chatter followed us. My complacent mind imagined that we might even come to play a part in an oral folk tale that will be passed on from generation to generation. And it could sound like this: Once upon a time there was a white baby prince. He was so small and delicate, his feet so fragile and clean, he wasn't allowed to walk. The gods gave him a seat on wheels, the funniest thing we had ever seen.

Us parading through the village bore a strange similarity to the festive parade that we had watched a couple of days ago in the center of Elmina. The people of Elmina township were excited to celebrate the *Edina Bakatue* Festival. It is celebrated in honor of the founder of the town, Kwa Amankwa, who accidentally discovered the Benya river, a tidal lagoon. Fetish priest, priestesses and herbalists ploughed through the dancing and cheering crowd while their pompously dressed chiefs were carried in elaborately carved wooden beds, very much like a matador after killing the bull in a Spanish bullfight. No bulls' ears or tails flew into the crowds, instead the heavy, golden necklaces and fine ornaments that the chiefs wore displayed their enormous wealth and their power. Gigantic umbrellas meant to enhance the chiefs' authority protected them from the sun as they greeted their loyal people with open arms and broad smiles.

Today's procession wasn't truly a royal one, but the delighted faces of humanity were just as unforgettable. The daily routine of the villagers' lives was interrupted. Dozens of little hands squeezed beside mine on the stroller handles. I didn't have the faintest idea, what must have been going on in Miles's head. He appeared to be content and not intimidated by all the smiling faces that looked down on him. I still wonder how much he actually noticed that he was the center of attraction. Was he listening to the language of the children? His inquisitive eyes were focused on something, but I couldn't figure out what. Perhaps he was looking at the pattern of the pair of shorts that walked in front of him, or the ragged red T-shirt beside him. His back was straight though, as if proud. The posture of a little prince!

Twenty odd boys and girls still walked, ran and skipped by our side long after we left the village. I fell in love with the innocent, newborn, frenetic joy that simple events evoked in these children and adults alike. That morning I wondered how we could bring some of those pure emotions back into our overly satisfied and overfed societies.

3
When in Ghana do as the Ghanaians do

'I keep the baby. He is my boy. How much do you want?' a female hand grabbed hold of my elbow and hindered me from walking past her.

Didn't these people have enough children as it is? What would they do with Miles? I wondered. Pass him around from open arms to open arms, inhale his smell, and then pass him back to me? Who knows?

We were something like celebrities in rural Ghana. We provided entertainment, injected variety into their lives, and we enjoyed it. Sylvia and I more so than Miles. People came too close to his face when they approached him. He coped, but I could tell that after a few days it started to bother him.

The Ghanaians were amused about our otherness. And, of course, we were easy to pick out. From miles away people saw our light hair, our fair skin, our different clothes and the golden locks of our baby boy. Any reason was good enough for the locals to initiate a conversation or simply a non-verbal dialogue. As soon as we slowed down our walking pace, hesitated for a moment or two, because we weren't quite sure how to react to the overwhelming friendliness, both women and men hovered over Miles. Women touched his tender skin, stroked his hair, pressed his nose, and basically annoyed him in an amicable sort of way. I never knew how serious the moms were when they threatened to buy Miles. I never tested it.

For outsiders like us it is hard to interpret the Ghanaians' mind. Everything seems to be said in a joking manner. Every action is accompanied by laughter. Stand-up comedians would love to come to this country. But are these people born like that? Maybe Ghanaian babies don't cry but laugh when they come out of their moms' bellies? You don't hear much whining from children, and if you do, then the surrounding adults laugh it off. A different way of growing up, a different philosophy about life.

In the Western World I often observe how parents rush to their crying children and console them, pampering them in a way that only encourages these rascals to happily cry again when they fall and when they don't get what they want. Kids enjoy creating scenes that give the impression that someone is about to cut their throats. Here in Africa it's different. Life is much too serious. You don't cry when you fall. Here, the one who laughs is the one who lasts.

Another typical street scene that involved us was, strangely enough, about the size of my breasts. Although I do wear the smallest bra size there is, women never thought it to be such an interesting topic as to discuss it in front of me in public. Here, on the West Coast of Africa, you not only talk about breast sizes in the streets, you point with your fingers at the breasts of other women. More than once African fingers pointed at my chest, then at my friend's chest, who has fuller breasts, then at Miles, and then back and forth again. My chest, Sylvia's chest, Miles, until we finally got the idea. What these startled ladies couldn't understand was why it was me who carried the baby. Why did I pretend to be the mother when it was obviously my friend who breast-fed him? Judging by my physique, I was the wrong person to carry the baby.

Again and again Miles's presence got us involved in the most intimate encounters with the locals. One beautiful morning we saw a handful of older women kneeling around an array of silver pots that were placed on the dusty ground in front of their mud dwelling. As we came closer, the heads of these women turned and, when they spotted Miles they got up. Using a local dialect and wild gestures they asked us to stay with them. I had a gut feeling that something extremely unpleasant was going to happen, but it was too late to run.

'Sylvia.' I introduced my friend with a shy voice and pointed at her.

Then I pointed at my son and said, 'Miles.'

One of the women pointed at me. I nodded and said, 'Stefanie.'

The ladies didn't say anything, instead they showed us the tattoos on their arms, endless rows of vowels with a few consonants. I smiled and thought if my name were of that length, I would also have tattooed it on my arm just so I wouldn't forget it. Our half-hearted attempts to pronounce their names caused a trial round of laughter. But that was just the beginning.

The hospitable womenfolk caressed Miles. Then they invited us for breakfast. We looked into the pots and saw raw fish. Sylvia jumped two steps back, making it very clear that she wasn't going to have any of the food. No doubt it was my turn. Raw silvery fish mixed with some unidentifiable paste at 7 a.m. made my stomach tighten and my head spin. Nevertheless, to decline wasn't an option because I would have deeply insulted their friendly gesture. My hand, not in any way monitored by my brain, reached deep into the challenging pot. I took a fistful of the stuff, shoved it into my mouth, closed my eyes and swallowed quickly. Had I been on the TV show Fear Factor I would have just made it into the third round, one step away from winning $50,000. Out here in Ghana there was nothing to be won. It was about being a traveler, not a tourist. Looking at the brighter side of things, I was testing the effectiveness of the hepatitis A vaccinations. As I mentioned before, there is a purpose for everything in life.

To complete the ceremony, a sandwich bag without the zipper, but filled with yellowish water and tied close by a knot, was presented to me. Grrr. Why wasn't I spared this drink? Just to get it over and done with, my fingernails ripped open one corner of the bag and I put it straight to my mouth. I drank a few sips, as the grandmothers launched into another storm of laughter, slapping their thighs in amusement. No. You must be kidding! I was meant to wash my hands with the water.

Later on that day, on the lookout for some fresh pineapple in order to cleanse what was left of my digestive system, we were stopped again. This time a group of middle-aged women wrapped in Ghanaian cotton prints took my hands and sat a turtle in them. To experience new things is the essence of adventurous traveling. The turtle was looking at me with its needle pin, dark eyes, as if to say: I am still alive. Please, don't eat me.

Was I supposed to eat the turtle? Not again. My appetite for Ghanaian dishes had been stilled forever. The ladies smiled at me encouragingly. Was I supposed to take the turtle with me? Was it intended to be a present? I had no idea. Maybe it was a present for Miles. But then again, do Africans keep turtles as pets? It didn't seem right. I must have stood there motionless for several minutes staring at the frightened reptile in my hand. I couldn't speak to these women in their language, so I shrugged my shoulders and returned the turtle to its owner. That must have been the last thing they wanted me to do. A gale of laughter broke out. Their bellies shook, their heads shook, their entire bodies vibrated. I responded with a quick smile, covered Miles's head with a sarong to protect him from the blazing sun, and disappeared in the masses. Honestly, what would you have done with the turtle?

One of our evening routines was to go for a stroll. The air was agreeably cool at the end of the day. We wound down. We explored our surroundings, saw and smelled new things. And pretty soon we learned that we weren't the only ones who cherished an evening routine. The very night that it was our turn to have a giggle about the peculiar ways of the natives, we were walking along the palm fringed, stunningly beautiful beach. At the sight of us a bunch of men jumped up in the air, abandoning their squatting positions as they stood ankle deep in the shallow ocean water. Trousers halfway over their behinds, they ran and hid behind the village trees. We had disturbed the 6 p.m. poop-session. Too late. The beach had already turned into an obstacle course. Ocean waves swept back what people wanted to leave behind, giving us no prior warning. We had to react quickly and jump, or else. The smell and sight stole the beach's appeal, luckily just for that time of the day.

All through our encounters with Ghanaians I lamented that I didn't speak any of the local dialects, but not once did I regret that I had taken Miles with us on this two-week vacation. He had his first contact with salty, cold ocean water and rough waves, he bathed every day in the two-foot deep swimming holes that I dug with motherly dedication into the sand, and he got a lot of attention from us and everyone else, maybe even a little too much.

For us, Miles had opened doors of contact that would have stayed closed had we been without him. We weren't primarily perceived as rich tourists, white women, wealthy exploiters. Above everything else – in the eyes of the natives - we were a mother, a child and a sister. We had something quite universal in common with the life of the Ghanaians, the mothers, fathers and the children that we met. The curiously bonding element of motherhood made cultural differences secondary. We provided a subject for later conversations in a harmless sort of way, never truly embarrassing for us and never intrusive for them, their families and their particular lifestyles. In fact, the Ghana experience encouraged me to visit Africa again with Miles, my passport to cultural eco-tourism.

4
Dancing in the Street

'Fete, fete.' He paused for a moment to take a deep breath then continued. 'Fete, fete, fete, fete.' The man who steered our taxi violently down the road had lost his mind. 'Fete, fete, fete, fete.'

I was certain not to be in France, otherwise I would have thought this madman was taking us to a party. All of a sudden he stuck his long finger out of the open window and pointed at a small urbanization, a shantytown afar with its aluminum roofs blinding your eyes in the afternoon sun. The streets were filled with people. Something was going on. Maybe it was a party after all, or a parade, or a wedding?

It didn't take long before we were stuck amid wildly agitating people and beeping cars. I kept telling myself, this couldn't possibly be the place where we want to go. We had hardly left town. Didn't the guidebook tell us that the hotel was quite a ways out of town and near a beach? I turned to Sylvia to check with her. She nodded. Something was wrong. We both leaned forward trying to explain to the excited young taxi driver that we want to go to a beach hotel, and the village close by it was called Gomoa Fetteh.

'G-o-m-o-a F-e-t-t-e-h,' my friend spelled out of the guidebook. He spoke only little English.

The reason why I hadn't bothered with learning Ashanti – the most prominent language in Ghana after English - was that you could never be sure if Ashanti would really help you. There are so many different languages and dialects spoken in this small country.

Sylvia said it over and over again: 'Gomoa Fetteh', not just 'Fete', 'Gomoa Fetteh.' Suddenly the young man realized that he had taken us to the wrong place. Needless to say he had told us the wrong fare. Just a few cents wouldn't get us to Gomoa Fetteh. He started to feel uneasy, a feeling that was going to increase later on as he struggled to navigate to the promised destination.

Clement was the young man's name. He was tall, skinny and nervous.

'You need to pay me 4,500 cedis.'

'Okay, no problem,' I had said.

He had asked for the equivalent of $5. Relieved and happy with the arrangement, he swerved through the crowds, flattening the odd pair of feet.

I aimed at enjoying my surroundings. It was a beautiful late afternoon. The termite mounds that bulged out of the earth threw golden dots on the five-feet tall grass. We followed a narrow track of sand. I noticed that our driver developed a tendency to stop for a few minutes at the unmarked intersections even though there was no traffic. Each time he looked around in bewilderment and mumbled to himself. It was obvious that he didn't know where he was going, but we couldn't help him either. Having been so determined in dictating the cost of the fare, he could hardly admit his problem now. In a way, I didn't blame him for feeling confused in this maze of tracks without any signposts, traffic, houses or people to ask. Nothing but a silent grass forest wherever you looked.

All of a sudden Clement stopped the car and demanded more money.

'Gomoa Fetteh is very far,' he said. Then he named his new price, which made me think I was about to purchase his car.

'No way,' I replied annoyed. 'The price is good.'

According to my sketchy map the hotel couldn't be that far away, but because we had been driving in circles for the last twenty minutes and he wasn't quite sure where to go next, it must have occurred to him that his car was using more gas than anticipated. For the moment, that wasn't my problem. Clement shot off, accelerating more than he should on these roads. If his skin hadn't been black I would describe his face as red with anger and frustration.

Then he started again. 'Gomoa Fetteh is very far. 20,000 cedi.'

This time he had lowered his rate considerably. I didn't respond. There was a stuffy silence in the car. Clement continued to drive recklessly and haphazardly. Soon it would be dark. My spirits began to sink and I was sweating, despite the cool wind that blew in through the half-opened windows. As far as I could tell we were in the middle of the grasslands with our prospective accommodation nowhere in sight, meaning no food, no drink and no bed for Miles. I looked over to Sylvia. She was calm, as usual.

My little boy had long ago thrown his bright yellow John Lennon sunglasses on the floor. His dark, trusting eyes looked awfully tired. He was crawling from my lap to Sylvia's lap, and back and forth again. I smelled a sour scent that came from his blown-up shorts. The trip was rough for him. He couldn't stand on his feet, yet he was dying to catch a glimpse of the outside world. He pulled my hair and yawned, refusing to sit down calmly. Why weren't we there yet?

Another intersection, and this time we saw some life. A handful of cone-roofed mud huts in the background and a tall young lady with a bucket on her head chasing a group of small children off the street. The driver steered close to her, and, I guess, asked for directions. Her arms pointed to the left, then to the right. Laughter. What on earth was going on? We drove off and our driver tried for the third time to renegotiate the fare. He grew furious at our stubbornness, but I didn't care, ultimately because it made him drive faster. Miles started to cry and I prayed for the blue sea to crop up in front of us. I juggled Miles with my eyes transfixed on the grassy horizon.

'Not long now, my sweetie, and we'll be there,' I reassured myself more than him.

And there it was, the flat concrete building on top of a small hill with a beautiful view over the wild ocean. Until today I'm not sure if this was actually the place we wanted to go to, but who cared then? The 20-room-hotel looked invitingly clean and of the minimum standard that we required for our travel companion who was still under the age of two.

Despite the good news, I quickly grew painfully aware of the inexplicably large number of cars on the parking lot. Then, legions of Asian families appeared from around the building with more than their fair share of children. How did they get here? How can this barely accessible place be so popular? It destroyed my hopes that we would end up with a bed for the night.

Sylvia hurried to the reception desk as if it would still matter, while I sat down on the batik cushions that were neatly fitted into the windowsills of the tiled entrance hall. Clement sat down next to me. I had given him a generous tip and he was a changed man within seconds. He was in no rush to get back to his town.

'Can I have your address?' he asked. He eagerly scribbled the PO box address of his brother in Winneba on a piece of paper.

'I never write English,' he explained modestly. 'But I learn English in school and I want write to you. Practice. Yes?'

I also understood that he collected postcards from all over the world. It is not in my nature to write to people whom I hardly know, and even less so to people who had annoyed me. Clement was an exception. Back home I actually wrote a few postcards to him. It was the teacher inside me who secretly congratulated his efforts to improve his English. I also contributed to his postcard collection and I remember that he wrote back once.

I am the driver who took from Winneba to Gomoa Fetteh on your rounds. I admired you and your little baby, so I collected your address. I will also like you to send a picture of the young baby. It is yours, Clement.

For now, I watched him play with Miles, who crawl-walked in large circles when I heard my friend say, 'They are fully booked for the weekend.'

'I can't believe this,' I said, even though I did believe it. 'What about a single room? We could all sleep in one bed, couldn't we?'

'I asked already. You see all these families here? They came from Accra for the weekend, and they have filled every single crack of the place like cockroaches.'

'But what in hell are we going to do now? We can't possibly return to Winneba.' I tried to imagine what the taxi driver's face would look like if we were to ask him to take us all the way back. I laughed to myself. 'Sylvia, let's have another look at your map,' I suggested. 'There is no way I am going back to Winneba, and I think everything else is even further away. But let's see.'

The two hotels in Winneba that we had already checked out were out of the question. One of them offered barren concrete rooms with no light, no plugs, no washbasins, nothing, and the other one was shut for refurbishment. While we discussed our Robinson Crusoe situation, the receptionist, a young girl, approached us.

'If you don't mind, our cleaning staff could vacate their room and you could stay in that room for two nights, then from Monday on we have plenty of rooms available.' She hesitated. 'The room has no private bath, it's very basic. You can have a look before you decide.'

I sighed with relief.

'Don't worry,' I said as fast as I could. 'We'll take it.'

Then I looked at the girl with honest concern. 'Where are the cleaning staff going to sleep?'

'We have a shed in the back garden. That's no problem. You are traveling with a small child. We can't let you go now. It is going to be dark soon'

The mother inside me felt impressed, the traveler inside me felt guilty, but certainly not guilty enough to refuse the room. A few moments passed and we were signaled that the room had been vacated. We walked around the back of the building, climbed up a few stairs, opened a heavy wooden door and dove on the only furniture in sight, three large beds.

Miles gulped down his milk. I force-fed him a few spoonfuls of abysmal tasting instant carrot and potato puree. Then we danced through the spacious room in our underwear. Five minutes later Miles was fast asleep, and surely dreaming about cooler days, tastier food and roller coasters.

Finally it was time for Sylvia and I to have dinner. We abandoned the hot box of a room that lacked any type of ventilation, fan or air-conditioning. Miles continued to snore at a safe distance from us. Every twenty minutes one of us would go to the toilet and check on Miles. It saved us from having to go to bed at six in the evening. Instead we were able to relax in the restaurant bar, a round open space with a thatched roof. To our surprise, local men occupied every single chair in this oversize tiki hut, except for the ones around the three dining tables. Squashed together, two sharing one seat, their necks craned in the direction of the TV. The small TV set was mounted high above their heads. Soccer was on. Brazil versus France. Hypnotized by the soccer match, none of them drank or ate anything. None of them looked at us while we ate. Hold on, let me say this again: None of them looked at us while we ate. Two white, female tourists in a bar and not one of the guys looked at us. There was a herd of men watching soccer but not one of them was drinking beer, shouting offensive slogans or hitting people with an empty bottle over the head. It was a peaceful party and everybody cheered for France.

Alas, an essential and significant experience of traveling is that gradually, day after day, your expectations are disappointed. Wherever you go situations will occur that erase your prefabricated ideas and shed a clearer light on the multifaceted humanity that lives on our planet.

The villagers who shared the tiki hut with us had walked about a mile through the pitch dark from their nearby homes that have no TV sets – and, for that matter, no electricity - to watch the soccer match and to socialize. I thought it extremely hospitable of the hotel owners to let their native neighbors hang out at the bar without consuming anything. They probably wished they could, but they had no money.

The next day Sylvia and I decided to explore the village where these men had come from. We took off after Miles had had his dinner. Belly full he rested content on my back, his legs swinging in rhythm with our leisurely walk. It took longer than I thought before we reached the small, small village built, in the shape of a ring on the edge of a cliff, with an amazing view. We discovered a row of carved out fishing boats, some finished, some still in the making. From afar we heard the famous sound of Ghanaian drums and singing. It seemed as if we would have our party after all.

A party indeed, but of an unusual nature. A funeral. Ghanaians don't mourn the death of their family members or friends in the same way we do. Death is the beginning of a new journey to the spirit world to meet one's ancestors. The Ghanaian tradition is to bury the dead in wooden caskets that resemble the deceased's trade, status or lifelong desire. Coffins may be fishing boats, cars or animals. They are colorful, not black and spooky shiny. When we arrived at the village we didn't see the coffin. We witnessed the aftermath of a joyous daylong celebration. A last hour of dance and music before the sun set.

Most of the dwellings in the village were pieced together from a random collection of wooden planks and aluminum sheets, leftover paint and cardboard, however, the reds, yellows and pinks of the laundry, the lush green of the plants and the theatrical presence of the people – all at home, speaking or singing with loud voices, organizing the evening meal, drink and bath – brought a romance to a community that otherwise would look poor and rundown. It resembled a naïve painting that was alive with three, four generations intermingling.

Sylvia and I were chatting about our past travel experiences, comparing them with Ghana, while we strolled along the one street. Curious children followed our footsteps, their eyes firmly fixed on Miles. Two respected elderly men sat gracefully and at peace with themselves, like Buddhists on a bench, under a fig tree. They were dressed in their festive garments, long robes with bright cubic patterns. They welcomed us and wanted to have their photograph taken.

Some fig trees later, a slim, gray haired man in his sixties shot like an arrow downhill at us. He grabbed my hands and danced with me to the rhythm of the drums. As awkward as I felt, I couldn't help but laugh. No doubt he must have had a little too much to drink at the funeral. His smile was the happiest smile that I have ever seen in my life. His shoulders heaved while he laughed and danced.

Miles was staring at him from behind my neck, his eyes widened in disbelief. What is this person doing with mom? Sylvia hurried to take a few snapshots. Soon after, the fun was over. A ranting, crashing voice yelled over to us. In the doorframe of a lime green wooden shack appeared a big, furious, almost wild looking woman. It was an easy guess, that she was his wife ordering him back into the house. And he obeyed. Like a squirrel he bounced up the path to his house, squeezing past his wife. He was still laughing because the alcohol had clouded his thinking, but his tough legs moved fast. They were afraid. They knew there was trouble ahead.

Right from the beginning I had had the strange feeling that the week we spent in Gomoa Fetteh would turn out to be delightful and special. Indeed, we met local culture first-hand and unspoiled. It was also an enjoyable time for Miles, besides the fact that he suffered from a nasty heat rash that covered his chest. There was a small playground on the premises, a huge cage with noisy, local birds, and a white, sandy beach to roll and play in. And Miles kept on walking around my deckchair until he managed without support. We were 100% content.

The only wish I was denied was the bike ride. We asked around in the village. Nobody had ever heard of a child seat for a bike, not even the local rent-a-bike-shack. What was I thinking, anyway? The athletic young Ghanaian who lived, slept and ran a rental out of a hut made from four fragile looking straw walls was so sorry that he couldn't help us out. He had three large bicycles for rent, but no child seat. He offered to take care of Miles, but no, that wasn't necessary, I said. We would have to leave in two days for Accra anyway. I could live without the biking tour. He promised to organize a car for us with a driver who would take us to Accra, and he would come along, too.

We returned to the Bellview Hotel, the same place we had started our vacation from. We sat in the courtyard, like on our first night, with the rental shack owner and his friend. The hotel staff played with Miles. We bought cigarettes and beer for our Ghanaian company, we talked and we laughed. Sylvia ate one of those meat kebabs from the street vendors. She wished she hadn't ... we had a flight to catch the next day.

5

East Africa
Food Talks

In many societies meat is more than merely food. In Kenya it's a status symbol. Here, eating habits make a statement about your wealth, your position in society and the importance of an occasion. Therefore, it seemed a hard call for my two-year-old to stick to his hitherto vegetarian diet. Meat, fish and rice are the cornerstones of any tourist's diet in East Africa. Where else in the world would you find a restaurant called *Carnivores* but in Nairobi? The restaurant's menu lists any type of exotic meat you can think of, with the exception of human meat: Zebra, gazelle, crocodile, giraffe and ostrich.

I remember that my African student friend Temi used to shake with laughter when we talked about vegetarianism spreading in Britain. She thought it was pretty crazy that someone who could afford to buy meat would deny himself the pleasures of eating it.

Even the Maasai, the lithe and fearless tribesmen who hate to slaughter their cows and goats, aren't strictly vegetarian. The handsome warrior tribe's principal diet consists of blood drawn from their cattle, goat's milk, berries and the meat of the game they occasionally hunt. The cattle blood gives Maasai men the strength to jump barefooted as high as a doorframe, putting our national basketball players to shame.

Arranging a fairly sugar-free life for my son was another one of those temporary away-from-home problems. Africans offered us cups of milky, over-sweetened tea. African children drink tea with caffeine and heaps of sugar at any age and any time of the day. Other popular drinks are Coca-Cola and Fanta, outdone in their sweetness only by the rolls of cream cookies that street vendors held in front of our faces wherever we stopped. Admittedly, I preferred those over peanuts and hard-boiled eggs.

Sometimes convenience rules over healthy choices and a good conscience. Miles and I traveled Kenya and Tanzania by local bus, by *matatu* – privately run minibuses driven by people who compete in ignoring traffic laws – and by car, in particular a rundown Isuzu 4x4 that I borrowed from a former teaching colleague who had moved to Nairobi. Since none of the vehicles were air-conditioned, and I didn't want to burden myself with a large cooler, it was most convenient to buy ice cold Fantas and sweets from the busy street traders.

Let's pause here, while I give you the picture of how Miles had changed since Ghana and how this affected our spontaneous

East Africa voyage. This time round my son was a more independent boy and, therefore, demanded more careful attention from me, vigilant eagle eyes, so to speak, that are able to look around corners and through table tops.

In Ghana I was the donkey-mom who carried Miles everywhere. This time round I was doomed to snail walk much shorter distances than I sometimes desired. Smart little Miles knew very well how to run fast without falling, yet he chose to demonstrate this skill always and only in the most inopportune circumstances. More than once did I have to chase after the runaway through suffocating bus stop crowds, the weight of our luggage pushing down on my shoulders. Having learned my lesson from the Ghana trip, I wisely abstained from taking a baby buggy to Africa. Consequently, Miles had to walk a lot. Although sometimes I couldn't help but take pity on his two little feet, like on that one afternoon when we returned to our car after a few hours of shopping in Nairobi.

Miles was so exhausted. We had been in and out of shops. Sidewalks and stores were so clogged with Africans you had to circle around. The heat and noise had worn us out, too. So I took Miles in my arms for the last stretch.

A middle-aged Kenyan man passed us, then stopped, turned around and said, 'Ma'am, you are spoiling your child. Let him *waaak*. He is old enough.'

I confess I was annoyed about his comment. What did he know about how our day had been and how much Miles had walked already? I guess it didn't matter to him. In East Africa two-year-olds aren't carried anywhere.

Miles's growing independence and understanding of the world around him gave me the feeling that we were really experiencing this trip together. At the age of two and a half a child's emotions become much easier to read. I had a much clearer idea about what Miles enjoyed and when he was scared or overwhelmed.

Miles was old enough to engage in play with other children, which allowed me to have a break from reading books to him and building sandcastles. Ten out of ten times the children he played with were locals who spoke a different language and who were black. Miles intermingled without apprehension or hesitation although he was fully aware of the obvious racial and linguistic differences. They didn't seem to matter in his play world. Kids are kids. Chase, hide-and-seek, soccer, and 'explore the world' are outdoor activities that cross international borders. In a perfect world, our focus on what we have in common rather than what draws us apart wouldn't change when we get older.

When we arrived in Nairobi I had no plan. To be honest, I had been more concerned with getting away from school politics, gas bills, immature au pairs and other related child care problems than thinking about what I was going to do in East Africa.

Kenya and Tanzania are traditional safari countries. Frustration hit me when I found out how pricey organized safaris are for someone who travels on a pretty short shoestring. Besides, no tour operator would take a two-year-old child on a safari. So, what was I going to do in the open plains, the dry grasslands of Eastern Africa? I could retreat into the small space of a beach hotel in Mombassa and escape from the challenges of distant travel, unbearable heat, no shade, dry throats and burning eyes. And what about Miles? Would he be up for all this, just in case I decided otherwise?

For practical matters in Kenya, I relied on those contacts that I had established before embarking on my journey. I stayed with a friend in Nairobi, borrowed his car, filled it with gas and took it upon myself to go on safaris with Miles. I accepted an invitation from a Kenyan family whose son I knew from back home. Later on, in Tanzania, I felt more confident and relied entirely on local transport, budget accommodation and people I met along the way for social contacts.

Despite all odds, there was one thing I had in my favor: Time. And time is what you need most of all when you travel with a child. Time to acclimatize, time to enjoy, and – in our case - time to become *au fait* with the East African way.

Initially Miles and I stayed at one of Kenya's International Schools, where my friend and colleague taught. The school was located between Nairobi and Thika. Since I had read Elspeth Huxley's memoir, *The Flame Trees of Thika*, a visit to Thika was high on my must-do list. One morning, Miles and I caught a ride with the school's English teacher to the secondhand market in Thika, a great place to buy the clothes that we wore once and that had been collected and shipped to Africa by nonprofit organizations. I found several cheap *déjà vu* jogging trousers and T-shirts amongst the huge piles of clothes, inexpensive and just right for a child's desire to be wild.

Thika is a pleasant town, unfortunately with far fewer flame trees than I expected. During my first days in Nairobi and the Thika area, when I still suffered from newborn anxieties, such as will I get ripped off, mugged or stabbed, I often thought about the six-year-old girl in the book who came to Africa with her mom and trekked out from Nairobi to Thika to join her father in early twentieth century Kikuyu country.

When Huxley arrived in Kenya, she and her parents had to face dangers of a different nature from the ones we face today. The challenges of pioneering settlers were the challenges of African witchcraft, sudden deaths, wildlife, self-help and home schooling. I admire the belief that these settlers had in their new life and the courage with which they faced the unknown. The more I thought about it, the less significant my own anxieties became. Nevertheless, I decided to avoid most of Nairobi at all costs.

Nairobi is a dangerous metropolis. Not a pleasant place for a tourist to hang out, let alone one with a child. The disastrously poor share their city with the wealthy and the many diplomats that live in walled, gated enclaves protected by armed guards. Violence flourishes. I had been warned not to drive into the city after dark or I might be shot in exchange for the car. One late afternoon, Miles and I returned from a shopping spree in one of the guarded Nairobi malls that cater for the rich, when we got an ugly taste of the disillusionment that turns Nairobi's inhabitants into angry people. On the road to Thika, past one of Nairobi's university campuses, demonstrating students threw stones at my car, nearly smashing the windshield.

Miles and I started our second week on the school's premises, a beautiful farm of several hectares with wild game roaming freely at a safe distance from humans. From talking to the staff, I understood that the property still belonged to the prestigious Kenyatta family, the family of Kenya's first president. We watered the dead-looking flowers in the mornings and miraculously brought them back to their colorful lives within seconds. We literally watched them raising their heads. We filled Miles's rubber boots with water, which was even more fun. We jumped around in the swimming pool in the afternoons, and shortly before sunset we would sit on the wooden bench at the lake. We picnicked and watched the more than 20 different kinds of feathered friends that descended from all directions, quenching their thirst from a long, hot day.

I tried to teach Miles how to use binoculars, an essential tool in East Africa, but without much success. He either looked at an object one foot away from him or he closed both eyes completely. However, against my belief, he reported having seen lots of interesting creatures and objects. So we both in our own little world – his blurry, mine clear - had a great time together on these cool evenings at the end of the dry season.

In East Africa the horizons seem to be further away than everywhere else in the world. Wide, open lowlands surrounded us. The dust of the red earth, the small heads of leaf-eating giraffes looking anxiously over silver gray acacia tree tops, the blood red and orange sky. Without a doubt, this is the East Africa we know from the movies.

This is the East Africa that I wanted to see. The other East Africa, the deadly tension in Nairobi, the 13-year-old street children, who bring up six or seven younger siblings since their parents died from AIDS, the poverty caused by imperial exploitation, mismanagement, corruption, and habitat destruction, I was also going to see. It deeply affected me. It saddened the adult in me who understands the relationship between cause and effect, and who knows that only the human is to blame for this catastrophe. I was glad Miles didn't perceive the other East Africa in the same way I did.

It is difficult to see the sad Africa from a child's perspective. People don't show their sadness. I didn't see any of the gray, stressed, 'don't-dare-speak-to-me' kinds of faces I would encounter in a German or American subway.

For Miles the highlights of our stay at the school were mealtimes. Miles and I were welcomed to eat with the students and to dig into the teachers' buffet. The fish and meat selection for the upper class African school children and their teachers was irritably vast.

Within no time my son had conquered the heart of the school nurse's daughter Lisette. The plumpish eight-year-old Kikuyu girl taught Miles table manners religiously and made sure he would eat up. Miles soon got the hang of mealtime routines. With plate in hand he waddled up to the nose-high tables covered in stiff, white tablecloths and served himself with whatever his small hands were able to reach, except vegetables. My little son had the time of his life.

Nyama choma – barbecued meat – the national dish of East Africa, so it seemed, is consumed with utter passion. Hence, observing an African eating chicken is as fascinating as watching a talented magician pull rabbits out of handkerchiefs. Chicken bones disappear completely in their mouths and, after some chewing, reappear shinier than the plastic bones of the school's skeleton, a trick Miles copied with great aplomb from Lisette. In fact, any meat bone that happened to get into his hands dropped back on his plate polished and waxed, after he had devoured every edible atom there was. No dog could ever dream of winning a bone nibbling competition with my son.

At one of those sociable dinners, the history teacher's wife who sat opposite us wouldn't stop talking about her last placement in Malawi. I leaned back. My ears listened to life in Malawi, my head nodded politely at short intervals, my eyes, however, kept track of Miles's appetite. I counted one fish, two fish, … seven fish, when my eyes popped out in a cartoonish fashion. Where did my gobbling toddler put the seven fish? I visualized two of those middle-sized fish filling his belly, three extending it, four causing stomachache, and the fifth one making him throw up … Nothing like that happened. They just disappeared quietly and obediently once chewed up by his tiny, rounded milk teeth.

Somehow Miles might have sensed that the all-you-can-eat buffet was an opportunity whose days were numbered. Soon, there could be dire straits ahead. I admit he was right. Only once more did the happy chance to saturate our bellies with a lavish amount of food reoccur, and that was during the negotiations about the dowry that the brother of a friend would have to pay after marrying his African bride – an important ritual that takes place before the actual wedding. Miles and I witnessed the negotiations in the heartland of Kenya.

The key to being invited to such a traditional ceremony was my friendship with a Kenyan student I met at the Teacher Training College in England. One year after I had finished my training as a Foreign Language teacher, and a few weeks before I was ready to leave for Kenya, I pinned my phone number on the notice board of the college in the hope that one of the many Africans that I had seen walking in and out of the building would be brave enough to give me a crash course in Kiswahili.

Vincent rang. A sharp, generous and emotional Kenyan in his late thirties. Back in those days he was terrified and suspicious of his new environment. He alternated between the four walls of the lecture theatre, the library and his dorm. He was lonely and, therefore, delighted at the prospect of sharing his culture with a Westerner. He decided to teach me for free.

At our second meeting he brought a gift along, a homemade tape that started with a thoughtful introduction about the spread of the Swahili language from Lamu and Zanzibar all over Eastern Africa. It continued with typical foreign language textbook versions of 'Hello. How do you do, Mr. Brown?' and finally changed over to mundane vocabulary like barbecued meat, fish, fruit, house, table and the numbers. It was the perfect present. I locked my bedroom door and rewound the tape a million times without embarrassment.

In exchange for this touching gesture I tried to make him forget the distance between his country and my dining room. I cooked rice and chicken, I bombarded him with questions about Kenya and promised to visit his family once I was out there. During our last meeting Vincent gave me an envelope that contained money for his mother. He trusted me to deliver it safely and in person.

From the very day that Miles and I set foot on Kenyan soil Vincent's mother, Rose, had kept her master bedroom, a Spartan concrete room with blue walls, a broken window and a large bed, converted into a guestroom for us. She and her husband shared the bed in the only other bedroom with three children in anticipation of our visit. At that moment in time Miles and I were still over 200 miles away, with no intention yet to abandon our first sojourn.

In rural East Africa there isn't such a thing as an announced visit. Telephone connections are rare. Every once in a while government officials go around collecting substantial amounts of money from the local farmers with the promise that their houses will be hooked up to phone lines and electricity. Promises that soon evaporate into nothing.

Being a spoiled, modern brat who is used to communicating via email, telephone or fax I couldn't imagine the sacrifices Rose and her family made. Therefore, I was in no hurry to visit. Instead, Miles and I went on a few safaris, with the result that I started being afraid of driving on Kenyan roads in the old 4x4 Isuzu. One of the reasons was that I got lost several times. Kenyan roads and towns aren't signposted. You can only guess where you are. Frequently, we gave lifts to people who hiked from town to town. Their names for the towns differed from the ones on my map. To add to all the confusion, many Kenyans find it hard to estimate distances between places. Not surprisingly, as they walk or cycle everywhere. A day's walk is just a few minutes by car, but how would they know?

The rapidly increasing number of rattling sounds that spat out of the Isuzu was the second reason for my apprehension. Unfortunately, my knowledge of cars was limited to the regular exercise of an oil change. The thought of breaking down in the middle of a dry and shelterless nowhere with a toddler in the back frayed my nerves. But there was no way I was going to disappoint Vincent's family and cancel my visit altogether. I glanced at the envelope for Rose that was still sitting in my backpack, a little creased, waiting to be delivered, and waiting for me to dismiss my fears.

The sight of Embu came as a relief. Flanked with gigantic jacaranda trees blooming in transparent blues and purples the road in and out of this town looked like an archway to a better place. I knew we must be close to our final destination.

The area around Embu was green and fertile. We passed neatly arranged *shambas*, small farms where coffee, banana, yam and pineapple grew, a joy for the eye of the traveler whose vision is blurry from driving over dusty dirt roads. Twenty minutes later we approached Ena, a small farmer's community. I had been advised to ask here for directions to the family's farm. How do you give directions through a maze of *shambas* without the convenience of street names? Everything looked the same to me. I ticked all the right and left turns off my scrap paper list. And there it was: Rose's blue house nestling among small hills.

Everyone in the garden rose to their feet as soon as our car came bumping along the uneven pine alley. The women stroked the creases out of their skirts. A tall, white haired, attractive looking man with perfect teeth, who must have been in his seventies but looked fifty-five, and who I guessed to be Vincent's father, peeled out of the crowd to welcome us. There was no need for Miles and me to introduce ourselves. Everyone knew who we were, since Vincent's letter had spoken about our visit to Kenya, and white visitors are few and far between on the local *shambas*.

Barely ten minutes after our arrival Vincent's father, Robert, jumped in the car wanting to drive to the local butcher. His gestures with my car keys were those of an amateur driver. I pushed myself to spoil his childish delight about sitting behind a steering wheel and directed him to sit on the passenger seat. He sighed theatrically. However, his great Isuzu moment came when we passed the first neighbors and he made damn well sure they became witnesses of his joy. He craned his neck out of the window greeting everyone with a beaming smile.

We bought the last pounds of meat that sat forlorn, adorned by flies, on the butcher's counter and returned home. Our first meal in Robert's house was going to be a welcoming feast. And a feast meant rice, carrots and, above all, meat. In the meantime, Rose, an enormous woman with a winning smile, had taken great joy in looking after Miles, who hadn't expressed any desire to join us on the way to the butcher. It always startled me how children trust certain people from the very first moment they meet.

As I nosed around the house I couldn't fail to observe that there was no running water, no toilet and no electricity. I cleared my throat, prepared to cheerfully cope with everything that awaited me. The fact that Miles and I ended up staying several weeks longer than the three days originally planned indicates that luxuries rarely triumph over human warmth.

We had a fabulous time. The weeks allowed me to gain some astonishing insights into life without the conveniences of modernity, the role of the woman in a still somewhat polygamous society, and the way people cope with situations that occur due to tough and demanding living conditions, situations that we would find impossible to handle. Weeks that allowed Miles to gain even more astonishing insights into the science of milking cows and goats, coffee growing and spending the evenings without electric light, color TV and books. It taught him to adapt to inflexible meal and wash times, and, most importantly, it showed him that life just isn't the same for all kids.

You get used to a lot of things in East Africa. I got used to looking after a hair-raising dirt ball on two legs who at times I barely identified as my son. One minute I would find Miles sitting on a pile of coffee beans listening to his personal stereo, the next minute I would drag him out of a smoke filled hut, the charcoal kitchen, dust covering his ears and nostrils, the color of his arms and legs hardly distinguishable from his new playmates, Rose's grandchildren Hector, Paul and Geoff. I was desperate to give him a good scrub or to spray some anti-bacterial Windex on his hands.

Every evening at five the maid, a skinny and wild looking woman with uncombed hair and in ragged clothes, would return barefooted from a nearby creek. She carried buckets of water that she heated over an outdoor fire. I was told it was my time to use the bathroom, a concrete cell with a hole in the bottom corner of the wall, which I figured must be the drain, and a stool. On the stool sat a bucket with boiling water, too hot to wash my hair with and too heavy to lift in any case. So I quickly gave up on shampooing my long hair.

In the darkening twilight Rose called the children into the house for an evening bath. Robert lit kerosene lamps. We sank into soft sofas covered with crochet blankets. Each adult had a child on his lap, a washcloth in one hand and a bowl of water in front of his feet. It was time to get clean and to listen to stories, to sit together and cuddle. Without a radio or TV running, time seemed to be standing still.

The next morning, out on the farm, Rose was picking coffee. Miles and I helped putting the red and orange coffee cherries into baskets whilst leaving the yellow and green ones to ripen on the coffee bushes. Rose confided in me - the woman and mother. She talked fast and cheerfully about her worries, like someone who had long given up trying to change the world.

Rose was the third wife of her husband. I asked her if she minded, but she didn't. It was a useless exercise to try and trace jealousy in her words. She was lucky to be the youngest of the three wives, she explained, which meant that Robert lived with her. But, to his disgrace, he would spend much of the little retirement pension that he received from the Kenyan Wildlife Service on booze, she complained. Often she was left without funds for gas, meat or medicine. She shrugged her shoulders and laughed. Then she told me how difficult it was for her grandson Geoff to attend elementary school.

'We have to employ a young guy from the area full time, and it is costing us a lot of money. He gives Geoff a lift to school on his bicycle, then he comes back to pick up Geoff's hot lunch and takes it to school. In the early afternoon he cycles for a third time to the school. He picks Geoff up and brings him home,' she explained.

I listened, convinced that the young chauffeur on his bike wouldn't make more than a few cents per day. And I wondered how Geoff would get to school during the rainy season, when the roads turn muddy. Then I thought about the children I had taught in the past, how they hated school most of the time and would have never seen it as a privilege to be in a classroom. I felt far too ashamed to tell Rose about it.

One morning during our second week on the *shamba*, Rose woke us excited and flustered, a little embarrassed, too.

'We need your help,' she whispered with a smile.

'Our son Patrick wants to get married. Our clan has to prepare a party for the bride's clan in order to get their

approval for the marriage. We must offer plenty of good food,'
she insisted.

From that morning onward I was scheduled to drive the ill-
mannered Isuzu up and down remoter than remote country
roads, transporting goats and grandmothers who were well
over 90 years old, cases of Coca-Cola and, of course, Patrick
and his mom to make arrangements for the big day. Miles
tagged along on all those trips, sometimes excited and
entertained by the people and animals, other times resentful
because he was bored or too hot. Several times I wanted to say
something to Rose about how these trips might be too stressful
for Miles, but in a world of constant struggle, it seemed almost
ridiculous.

Finally, the countdown began. Two more things needed to be
taken care of: Shopping in Embu and arranging the exact date
for the celebrations with the bride's father. Our visit to Embu
was the more pleasant of the two trips. We chased for hours
from stall to stall up and down the steep open-air market. Rose
wanted to buy several tons of rice. We compared prices. A
difference of two cents per kilo mattered. We also bought large
sacks of carrots and plantains. Weakened from the running
around, I catapulted Rose and Patrick into one of the local
restaurants for lunch. I used the restrooms with Miles, thrilled
by the opportunity to wash his hands and face in the middle of
the day.

When we were ready to leave, trouble started. A handful of
street children had thrown themselves in front of the Isuzu,
pretending that I had run them over, or at least hurt them.
Their begging hands stretched out in front of my car window.
Other sticky hands clung to the side mirrors and door handles.

Desperate faces pressed their noses against the glass windows staring at Miles, the healthy and protected boy, in anger and envy. I almost felt guilty for having cleaned him up.

Homicidal insanity surrounded my vehicle. Unfortunately, the glue sniffing, abandoned, wasted lives of young children were a common, yet giddy sight in Kenya's towns. A sight Miles and I didn't comprehend, each of us in our own way. I didn't comprehend why we, as a human race, allow this to happen. Miles didn't comprehend the children's anger. He realized that these children were different. Their voices were demanding, their eyes stared carelessly and their hands were grabby. He perceived them as a threat to his mother because they would hassle me for money. In the streets of Nairobi I observed how he pushed children much taller than him out of the way to protect me. Each time the look on his face was stern. The low threshold of children who had nothing to lose felt threatening. I saw the need to reassure Miles that they were poor and had no mom and dad, yet they were harmless children. I hoped he didn't sense my alarm.

The next day we maneuvered along a zigzag road to the farm of the bride-to-be's family. I could have sworn we were driving along a dried out riverbed and not a road. Gas pedal all the way down, we conquered sand hills, sliding from side to side without getting stuck.

'Next time I do Kenya in a Land Rover,' I thought to myself.

Still only halfway there, I couldn't shake off my dread of the return trip. What if something broke on the car? We hadn't come past any living creature on our way. We were lucky enough that I hadn't run out of gas as yet. Still it seemed that I would barely make it back.

The bride-to-be was nervous as hell. There was something about her I didn't like. Perhaps it was the firmness with which she spoke and sat on the rear seat, a firmness that one could easily confuse with ruthless stubbornness. Her father, who we needed to talk to, had gone out for the day, hunting or something, nobody knew exactly. We waited for hours. Then we started to run out of daylight. I urged Patrick to leave and suggested we come back the following day. The headlights of the Isuzu didn't work properly. We would hardly be able to see much in the dark. But Patrick didn't have much say on the farm of his bride-to-be, a perdurable Kenyan etiquette. And she was determined to wait for her father no matter what the cost. Intentionally, she ordered her mother to prepare sweet, milky teas, so we had to stay. But I was ready to go and ready to kill her. When I insinuated a farewell, Miss Future Bride screamed at me, making shrilly sounds.

'You are such a rude woman. In Kenya it is impolite to refuse tea. You don't know how to treat us people.' She eyed me with unconcealed hatred.

I gave up, drank the hot tea and burned my mouth. The weary Westerner inside me felt utterly uncomfortable, but there are limits to everything. Miles needed to get home safely, now. We left. I never found out how Patrick communicated with her father since we never went back until the actual day of the ceremony. And, to tell you the truth, I wasn't that interested.

Miles sat on Patrick's lap in the passenger seat. Six women, tons of rice, carrots, bananas and a paranoid goat, a donation from Patrick's grandmother, filled the back of the Isuzu. How? I don't know. What I am about to describe wasn't a leisurely drive along Miami's beachfront – we were back on the road from hell: destination the bride's farm.

The women who were squashed in the back of my car, and who must have been butt-sore after just five minutes, chattered and laughed nonstop. There was a good reason for their cheerfulness that I only grasped later when we passed many of the other guests who had to walk. They must have left well before the sun had come up. Walking sticks cut through the hot air greeting us. Everybody smiled. Everybody was looking forward to the party as they trudged on, the already hot morning sun shining on their backs.

In the rear mirror I saw all six women wrapped up in their sarongs in a Muslim fashion. Once we arrived they popped like butterflies out of their cocoons that had protected them from ending up like me, red and dusty.

I was allowed to look red. I was allowed to walk around and take photographs instead of peeling plantains. The men who had been busy slaughtering posed in front of the cow that now hung from the tree. The elderly womenfolk posed in flowery dresses on flowery sofas in the shade of a giant bamboo. They smiled into the camera, their hard-worked backs still straight. Perhaps they were remembering the time when they got married themselves. It was their silence that set the solemn atmosphere. No word was spoken between the two clans.

Miles and I went for a walk. We watched how the younger women of Patrick's clan were boiling the meat for the almost 100 guests on coal fires next to the main farmhouse. We had a look at the grunting pigs. Then Miles saw his three playmates, Paul, Hector and Geoff. He joined their game of pushing a wheel with a stick along the ground, kind of like a horizontal yo-yo.

Good cooking and plenty of meat was an essential part of the appeasement strategy applied by Patrick's kinfolk, who aimed at negotiating a low dowry. The bride's clan was served first. Paper plates filled with gigantic mountains of meat and rice moved from hand to hand. The cheeks of the Kikuyu faces bulged outward, as if someone had pushed two golf balls into their mouths. Suddenly, talk interrupted the chewing sounds. The bride's clan had opened the conversation, an obvious sign of digestive satisfaction.

With well-upholstered bellies, the members of each clan got up, one at a time, and introduced themselves to the other clan, explaining in Swahili in what way they were related to either the bride or to Patrick. One of Patrick's cousins, a policeman from Mombassa, took it upon himself to be my interpreter, and it was also him who urged me to stand up and to enlighten the curiously peering crowd about Miles's and my connection to Patrick's family. After my short speech the heads of the elderly nodded approval.

Then, everyone who had something to say on behalf of either one of the couple to raise or lower the dowry stood up and spoke. The bride and Patrick sat silently and seriously on wooden stools in-between the two clans, as if they were in a courtroom, with two bottles of Coca-Cola, the Kenyan champagne it seemed, behind them on a table. Their faces betrayed nothing of the emotions they felt.

Patrick was an educated young man who would laugh and joke with me about the old Kenyan ways. Nairobi had given him a modern outlook on life. During the week he attended computer science classes in the Kenyan capital. But when he was in the countryside he succumbed to traditional life.

Somehow I think he was smart enough to mix both worlds to his advantage.

The negotiations were going well in his favor. All of a sudden, the parents of the couple and the eldest from each clan got up and retreated into the farmhouse. They had heard enough. The final decision was imminent.

Whereas I, the adult, was captured by the cultural experience, the day turned out to be too long for Miles. He was restless. He had run out of ideas for play. He was also tired from the heat and refused to sit on my lap. He was running around aimlessly when a huge, ugly turkey – aren't all turkeys ugly? – surprised him from behind and then chased him around the courtyard. Miles cried. I felt like calling it a day and going home, but, of course, I couldn't. The turkey somehow took a liking to Miles. It didn't matter how many times I chased him away, he would swing back like a boomerang, hunting the little boy. It was a purposeless battle between my tired son and a stubborn turkey. I wished they had slaughtered the bird and thrown it in the pot together with the cow's meat.

One of the many maids on the farm noticed the desperate expression on my face and she offered to make another sweet tea for Miles. She hit the turkey over its head with a stick and gave it a farewell kick in the side. She also brought some water so I could wash Miles's hands. In the end, Miles recovered and his energies came back for a final strike. He tried to make contact with a small girl in a frilly pink dress that looked as if it had been well worn by uncountable generations of one-year-olds. Miles grabbed her arm with the clumsiness of a toddler who should be in bed, when the girl burst out in tears for which there was no solace. Oh well, the afternoon hours really hadn't been easy for Miles. Eventually, I put him to sleep on the dusty car seats.

The farmhouse door opened, the guests gathered and the father of the bride announced the verdict: 2 large sacks of sugar, 2 cows, 44 goats and 300 dollars in cash. Wow. I was shocked. The price was astronomical. Bewildered, I looked over to Patrick, who in turn seemed relieved and happy.

On our way home he and I talked about the outcome of the marriage negotiations. To my astonishment he answered, 'Let me explain. I'm not meant to pay the whole sum at once. I have all my life to pay. You have to understand that once we are married she belongs to my clan and she won't see much of her family. Bringing part of the dowry every year or so to the farm gives us a good reason not to lose touch with her family.'

Then he added wittily, 'If I was to bring a herd of 44 goats to her farm tomorrow, the goats would starve, because her family isn't rich enough to feed them all at once.'

Back at Rose's I retreated immediately to my room. I laid on my bed exhausted but still awake, thinking about this big day. For me it had been a testimony of family politics and economics, not of love.

I never saw the couple kiss, hug or show any signs of affection to each other during the time I had spent with them. I began to wonder whether the notions of romance and affection aren't notions of the privileged rich of the world, who can choose to marry the people they truly love regardless of social and economic status. Much later I learnt that the display of public affection is considered vulgar amongst the Kikuyu. However, marriage isn't entirely a personal matter. It's a contract that binds two kinfolk together, an invaluable component of the structure of Kikuyu tribal society.

I also thought about how the huge portions of cow's meat had lifted the spirits of one hundred people.

I also thought about how Miles had converted from a herbivore into a true carnivore who, until this day, prefers meat and fish to candy, and certainly to anything that's green.

6
Where the Wild Creatures Live

Toothbrushes and toothpaste flew out of my hand. Then I screamed in panic and pain. I hopped on my right foot in circles and shook my left leg as hard as I could. At the same time, my fingers dug into Miles's T-shirt and skin to prevent him from falling off my hip. My dance was a masterpiece of acrobatic clownery. Finally, the monkey let go. Very slowly, I placed my foot on the ground. My injured calf felt bruised and it hurt like hell, especially where the monkey's teeth had punctured the skin.

'Stupid monkey,' I moaned. 'Oh, how I hate them, these horrible animals.'

Miles gave me a sad look. He loved monkeys. How could mama say that she hates them? But, then again, he felt a little fearful himself. One of those monkeys had bitten his mother with its long, sharp, canine teeth.

Do not feed the Monkeys it said in bright yellow letters on wooden boards all over the campsite. Why, then, had the French herd of tourists come running with bananas that, surprise, surprise, attracted a large troop of vicious vervet monkeys? The French can read English, even though they like to pretend that they can't. After feeding bananas to the monkeys and taking snapshots, the French tourists had left the scene. Miles and I appeared. We came from brushing our teeth in the public washrooms. As we crossed the open campground, mercilessly, and without prior warning, a troop of furry creatures attacked us in the hope we also had bananas to give away. I grabbed Miles off the ground and struggled to fight off the craving monkeys with toothbrushes and toothpaste. Grotesque weapons of defense, if you think about it. This time, motherhood didn't evoke any sympathy, any feelings of mutual understanding. The monkey that decided to hang itself from my calf, its teeth deeply dug into the flesh, was a female with a baby on its back. It didn't care that I, too, was a mother with a toddler clutched to my hip. Terrified, I stared at the deep, red marks the monkey's teeth had left behind. The thought that monkeys, just like cats and dogs, transmit rabies shot through my head.

In retrospect, I have to confess that I wouldn't repeat any of our homemade style drive-thru safaris, whose outcome - good or bad – was entirely left to chance. Miles and I could have been eaten by lions and leopards, trampled on by elephants or got stuck with our vehicle in the middle of the thick African bush. Who knows if and when the park rangers would have come and searched for us? Until then, we would have had to sit in the choking air of our car, windows closed and hoping for the best. You wouldn't dare leave your car out there.

When Miles and I talk about the safaris today, he hardly remembers any of those few exciting moments when we actually saw game close enough so that we were able to distinguish a hippo from a rhino with our bare eyes. These moments were few and far between endless hours of sitting in a car, being exposed to the humming sound of the car engine, and having to breathe in exhaust fumes mixed with the dust that came flying off the red roads while we drove.

Perhaps we choose the wrong time of the year. Hemingway's green hills of Africa were light brown. Heat and filth dominated the setting. But as soon as the violent rains would put a fresh cover on the landscape and bring back to life the dormant roots, many roads were inaccessible for a while. Then, tourists would pour into the National Parks. Their tour vehicles would simulate a herd of zebras not only by their looks - many of those white safari buses carry black stripes - but also in number.

Fortunately, the monkey assault of Namanga, a small border town at the crossroads to the Amboseli National Park, happened after we had explored the park. Our return trip to Nairobi coincided with my mad rush to a Nairobi hospital, where I was administered the first of a set of five post exposure rabies shots. Better safe than sorry. I certainly didn't wish to die lying in the streets, trembling and raving like Edgar Allan Poe.

Despite its happy ending - I never suffered from hypersalivation, anxieties or confusion - I regret having told the story to my friends. It's peculiar how good friends take great pleasure in making fun of events that could have been fatal.

While we were still in the Amboseli National Park, Miles was in command of the vehicle. I had to give him something to do. He steered the car along the empty roads. That way, he would forget about the dust between his teeth, in his nostrils and between the elastic bands of his underwear and his skin. We were slowly maneuvering around a hill when I braked abruptly. A small herd of elephants was crossing the road. In the middle of the parade were two calves. The ponderous, tranquil animals didn't seem to be bothered by us. I was excited for Miles. The elephant is an animal whose size doesn't intimidate, maybe because of its big floppy ears and its slightly bent trunk, which looks like a playground slide. Every kid loves Jumbos, and so did Miles. We sat motionless in the car watching the heavy steps of those gray giants.

My eyes wandered beyond the mammal parade. They were met by the silhouette of Mount Kilimanjaro. Its white, snow-covered top was hardly distinguishable from the thin white clouds that surrounded the summit. It is the beauty of this perfect picture book mountain as a backdrop to the large concentration of big game that has made the Amboseli National Park such a popular destination.

There was no reason for the animals to hang out close by the road. We were lucky.

'Miles, quickly, look. There are some lazy buffaloes,' I said.

Miles jumped up and down and pointed with his finger through the open window, screeching, 'Mama, buffaloes, buffaloes.'

White cattle egrets, the buffaloes' lifelong companions, sat on their black, rounded backs. Herds of zebras and wildebeest surrounded us, easy to spot on the dried out, flat lake basin that makes for a large area of the park. A spotted hyena stared at us across the plain.

The afternoon hours in the park turned out to be very rewarding. I felt like we deserved it after the gruesome and aggravating 50-mile drive from the main road to the Meshanani Gate. The whole time I had been afraid that the gravel would split the car tires, and the thought of having to change tires in the midday heat on an isolated road, where the only people we might encounter were Maasai selling soccer ball-size ostrich eggs, didn't really appeal to me.

At sunset, we drove into the public campsite that was to become our accommodation for the night. It was protected by low-growing thorn bush. Miles was helping me pitch our tent when a young Maasai appeared from nowhere. He approached us quietly. He wanted a job as a night guard. I hired him. He was fine with the money and disappeared. Shortly before dark he would come back, he said, to protect us from trudging night elephants with his spear and the instinct of a herdsman.

I shut off the motor of the car. The silence of the evening, occasionally interrupted by the chirp of a bird, appeased our tired senses. So did the colors of the upcoming night. The sky turned bright red, then burgundy and purple. The leafless acacia trees spun their black arms across the setting sun. We huddled up close to the campfire and dug with our forks into canned food. Miles had been busy collecting branches and stones. Fascinated by the campfire, he approached the flames until it felt too hot. We spoke about the day and the animals. I was happy to have so much time for him.

All of a sudden the Maasai stepped out of the darkness. He was quiet, his English almost nonexistent. He nodded a lot. During the whole time that I attempted some conversation with him, Miles stared at the gap in the front of his teeth, a common feature among Maasai men. Before Miles and I retired for the night I offered the young guard a drink, some food and one of my sweatshirts. The air had cooled considerably and all he wore was a red blanket-type poncho thrown over his shoulders. I hoped that he wouldn't get too bored sitting all night by himself next to the campfire.

The world around us went quiet and I was exhausted, but I failed to relax completely. The traveler tales about elephants unintentionally trampling over your tent while you are asleep made me nervous. I wondered what the maybe twelve, at most fourteen-year-old, Maasai would do to scare them away. Perhaps he would just wake us in time and tell us to run as fast as we could.

An unusual sound woke me in the middle of the night. Was it an animal trying to pass through the thorn bush hedge, or had I been dreaming? I peeked out of my tent. Our guard was gone. I sighed. Somehow, I had anticipated that this would happen. I stared at the dying flames of the campfire, pondering about the work ethics of Maasai herdsmen, or rather how much they probably hated the idea of National Parks and the presence of tourists on their land, then I went back to sleep.

I might be stating the obvious, but it needs to be said that watching lions, monkeys and giraffes in a zoo is much less trouble for parent and child than going on a safari. The problem is that zoos have never appealed to me. Small, dirty cages with insane looking animals pacing up and down, sniffing their urine, and then pacing up and down again, all for the public's amusement. Even the cleanest and most humane zoo to me is anything but a peaceful place to enjoy nature on summer weekends. Zoos claim to celebrate animal diversity and to bring the visitors close to the animal. The latter they certainly do. The captive creatures are right in front of your nose, so close that you are glad they are behind steel bars.

Ironically, when on safari you expect a zoo-like behavior of wild animals that prefer to avoid humans rather than approach your vehicle for a quick pat on the back, and during nighttime you wish they were behind steel bars that hindered them from becoming unpleasant, even if their visit turns out to be something you made up in your dreams.

Imagine the lush green highlands of Scotland roaming with small antelopes, gazelles, lions and elephants. I couldn't give this spectacular park a miss, the famous Aberdare National Park, where Queen Elizabeth learned of her accession to the throne while she stayed at the luxurious Treetops Lodge. Needless to say, Her Majesty's trip would bear no comparison with our experience, for better or worse. First of all, our car got stuck in the tire-gobbling mud only two miles away from the park, near a remote entrance that I had never planned to go to. Had it not been for the four brave park guards who happened to pass by on their way home from work, Miles and I would have had to spend the night in the car and call upon our guardian angels to get us out of that mess by the following morning.

The park ranger at the lonesome gate entrance was more than surprised to see us. We entered his office, a concrete room with an old desk and an old radio. I paid the entrance fee and urged him to give us directions to the nearest *bandas*, simple huts that serve as accommodation for park visitors. Sunset was imminent, therefore he convinced me to stay at the much closer campsite. We would be fine, he said, and wished us a good time in the park. He walked us to my beat-up vehicle, said a cordial goodbye, and returned to his solitude.

The road took us up and down the undulating Afro-alpine moorlands. Here and there a duiker skipped across the road. Just before we reached the campsite I saw the shadow of a cheetah disappear into the dense bush that fenced off the road. I knew then that I wasn't looking forward to the night. I certainly didn't appreciate the sight of a cheetah shortly before I was going to pitch our tent on a lonely grass opening without any other campers around. I looked back to the hill where we had come from and wondered if the park ranger was watching us with his binoculars. For no particular reason I waved.

Miles and I crawled under the tent canopy that protected us from the dark, the drizzling rain and the creeping cold. We huddled up in our sleeping bags. I was frightened. Strange, how the presence of a two-year-old can comfort a thirty-three-year-old woman who is kept awake by unfamiliar sounds. We were camping in the home of cheetahs, leopards and lions. It is difficult to understand why some people like to take uncalculated risks. That night I was one of those people, infected with the incurable safari fever, the need to see wild game, no matter what the expense.

The rain stopped. Suddenly I felt the vapor of an animal close by. I heard the breathing. My heart was racing at an unusual speed. Convinced it must be the cheetah from earlier on, I quickly unzipped the tent and roared like a lion into the darkness. My hands were shaking when I closed the tent after my heroic action was completed. The embarrassing roar might have frightened a few ducks or chicken. And it wakened and frightened Miles.

'Mama, what is it?' he asked, his eyes wide open. 'Is it a lion?'

'Shhhhh,' I whispered and put my finger on his and my mouth. 'No, it's not a lion. Just be quiet for a moment.'

I held his warm little hand in mine. Mine was the one shaking uncontrollably while we listened to the chewing sounds of a wild living being right next to our tent. Determined to find out what it was that was keeping us prisoners of our own fears, I opened the tent door one more time. I looked into the big, round eyes of two duikers, which stood alert and motionless just a couple of steps away from me. Semi-relieved, I turned around to look at Miles. Could it be true? He had already fallen back asleep. Fortunately, he didn't understand the potential danger of such animals that are depicted in children's books as furry and cute, with smiles on their faces. I slept like a dog that night, half of my senses on alert, the other half getting some rest.

The next morning we had breakfast on the dew-coated grass. I boiled some water for tea, and we had crackers with peanut butter. I gave Miles one of my fleece sweaters to wear. The morning was unexpectedly chilly. From our comfortable observation spot, we watched a lonesome elephant crashing through the dry branches of a forest that had been deprived of its leaves by a fire. After breakfast we drove through a large bamboo forest, over streams abundant with fresh water, and we saw large fairy tale trees with moist bark and mossy beards.

I thoroughly enjoyed the scenic beauty of the park, forgetting the images of stalking cats in the darkness, ravenous for meat, until I read that lions in this park had killed two men in the past. One had been attacked by a lion on his walk to a nearby waterfall, the other one on his way to the outdoor restrooms of a lodge.

Despite of this, the safari tourist in me still couldn't get enough. Just one more park, I kept saying to myself. I knew I was selfish. Miles would only enjoy the mornings of our safaris. In the afternoons he would get tired of sitting in the car, especially when there were no animals to look at. And I wasn't as rich as Queen Elizabeth. Besides, I would have felt out of place staying in a $250-dollar-a-night lodge. Besides, Miles loved the freedom that comes with camping.

Another day, another park. Trouble free, we arrived at the Enjoro campsite in the Nakuru National Park, about 100 miles northwest of Nairobi. We had already caught a glimpse of what the park is famous for, its salt lake covered with pink flamingos and white pelicans, although their number has been decreasing in recent years. I was driving slowly underneath the roof of yellow acacia trees, looking for a nice spot to set up our tent. The car was still in motion when a small monkey rocketed through the window and leaped onto Miles's lap. It snatched the apple he was chewing out of his hands and exited the car via the window on the other side. Miles was in such shock that he forgot to cry about the loss of his apple.

A few minutes later, barely recovered from the event, he called me with urgency. 'Mama, look, another monkey.'

I was busy unloading the car. I craned around to look in the direction of his voice when I saw the enormity of a fat and furry baboon close by. Now, these monkeys can't be taken lightly. Just a glance at their long canine teeth makes you want to escape from the scene. Before I could interfere, Miles had walked up to the monkey. Both of the same height, the monkey sitting, Miles standing, they stared at each other. A hair-raising shot for the candid camera. I freaked.

'Miles, come back. Miles, please step back slowly. Don't run. Miles, listen, please.'

I yelled moderately, far too frightened to approach the animal myself. The baboon yawned, displaying the sharp teeth that framed its bright pink, rectangular-shaped tongue. Fortunately, the sight of it made Miles feel unsure about his adventure, and any possible intention of stroking the animal vanished from his mind. He ran toward me, tears in his eyes.

Only five minutes later, a curious warthog decided to pay Miles a visit. The poor boy was picking up some firewood when he suddenly looked into the menacing face of this animal, larger than him. Miles jumped into my arms. The warthog danced away, its ridiculously skinny tail straight up in the air.

I decided that three encounters of that caliber within less than twenty minutes must have been nerve-wracking even for a child like Miles, who adores all of those four-legged beings with the naïvety of a two-year-old.

I organized a local guy to guard our tents, just in case the baboons were planning a burglary. Although we kept anything eatable in the car, those curious monkeys are known for ripping tents apart just to peek inside.

Miles and I climbed into the safe Isuzu, rolled the windows up and drove to Nakuru Lake. It was exactly one hour before sunset. Cormorants, greater and lesser flamingos, yellow-billed storks, ibises and great white pelicans bordered the banks of the lake and adorned the nude branches of trees in the mustard colored evening world. A yellow-billed stork approached our car and I was lucky to get a great close-up shot. And there it stood, a pre-historic looking mammal, a leftover from the dinosaur age. A white rhino surrounded by hundreds of feathered creatures. Transfixed, we admired the animal.

The next morning we drove past viewpoints with names like Baboon Cliff and Lion Hill and I managed to spot a lot of game. Grazing herds of zebras, shy impalas, warthogs and waterbucks. Miles decided that the waterbuck, with its soft, long coat, looked like an animal out of the toy store. He wanted to take one home. The Nakuru Park experience was certainly unique and well worth it for both of us, had I not got lost in the thick euphorbia forest. I usually have a good sense of orientation and I am very capable of reading maps, so I really haven't got a clue what happened. I guess I must have taken the wrong turn with the park exit already in sight, and there we were on a mud track that snaked into a series of tight turns, walled on both sides by thick greens. Any moment I expected a wild beast to step out in front of us. I prayed that we wouldn't get stuck because there would have been no way that I would have opened the doors of the car. If I remember right, the car inched along for about an hour until we finally got out of the forest onto the open plains. And, sure enough, the original well-intentioned plan to make it a short day for

Miles had failed again. It wasn't the first time that he had to be brave and occupy himself by looking at books or out of the window, eat and sleep, but it was the last time, I promised.

'We'll go on one last safari,' I told Miles. 'One more time we'll go, but not in a car. We'll walk. We'll do the real thing.'

After having left Kenya, Miles and I spent several weeks in Arusha, a town in Northern Tanzania. It is a safari mecca and the gateway to the Serengeti. A few miles out of town there is a campsite run by a Scottish couple and a bunch of Maasai, a fun place to be with a child. For us two it was about time that we took a long break from moving around.

Our tent became our bedroom; the restaurant that served delicious homemade pizza became our self-service kitchen; the communal showers with the hot water for as long as you were amongst the first to turn up became our bathroom; and the playground, the volleyball field, the grassy areas surrounded by bougainvillea hedges became our garden and playroom.

Our new retreat wasn't a lonely place. Every day we made new friends. One day the owner of the campground invited us to play with the puppies at his house up in the hills. On other days we visited rose farms with a flower dealer from South Africa. But above all, Miles felt attracted by the company of the Maasai who guarded the place. Many times I would find him spending his time alongside one of these tall, skinny warriors.

Verbal communication surely wasn't what kept Miles in their company, since these traditional cattle herdsmen didn't speak any English or German. Was it their peacefulness that attracted him? Was it the comradeship amongst them? Was it the nomadic lifestyle that he somewhat shared with the Maasai and that wasn't based on belongings and many words. Obviously, there was no need to speak for the tiny white boy and the tall black man that I watched for hours through the netted door of my tent. Together they sat on the grass, Miles imitating the proud pose of the Maasai. They listened to the sounds that came out of a transistor radio, and they chewed on blades of grass.

On one of those tranquil days, our friend Nigel from South Africa persuaded me to accompany him on a walking safari in the Mount Meru National Park. Initially I was surprised that he invited us, since Miles and I had given him the shock of his life the previous day, an experience that cemented Nigel's views on bringing up children for the rest of his life. I had made an irrational attempt to potty train Miles by dressing him in a pair of shorts but without a nappy. Miles made it to the toilet a few times during the day, however, on the way back home from one of those rose farms he kept quiet and did his big, smelly business on the rear seat of Nigel's car. I was so embarrassed, particularly when I saw the disgust on the face of a young man who probably never liked children in the first place but who would hate them from now on.

I smiled and said in a consoling way, 'I will clean it all up.'

He pursed his lips and I expected the worst. 'Okay. Go ahead,' he said and left me with the car keys.

A week later he told me that the seats in his car still smelled foul. And years later, when I emailed him that I was going to write about my travels with Miles, he made damn well sure that he reminded me again of the incident.

'I hope you will mention the accident that happened in my car!,' he wrote. Here, Nigel. I have done it.

But a walking safari, that really sounded like fun, something different, anyway. And since Mount Meru National Park was just around the corner, Miles and I agreed to join him.

This time my little boy enjoyed every moment of it. We hiked the park with a guard ranger, who carried a rifle to protect us from charging buffaloes. Nigel and I alternated in carrying Miles on our shoulders. Miles missed no chance to investigate the round hills of buffalo pooh with a stick and with the soles of his shoes. We touched and smelled nature.

For once we were able to move around quietly, become one with nature, and the persistent sounds of a car engine wouldn't give us away. We stalked through the high grass like leopards until we saw a herd of giraffe only a few feet away from us. We felt so small as we stood next to their long legs. Then they turned around and bolted off.

We spent this fabulous day at the foot of Mount Meru. It was also at the foot of Mount Meru that I saw my husband-to-be for the first time. Two weeks later we met again on Zanzibar. At the foot of Mount Meru I reflected again and again about the possible virtues of going on driving safaris with a toddler, and in my mind I ended up voting against them. Mount Meru is the impressive mountain that guards the Maasai campsite. It is the mountain that watched Miles wade through the mud in heavy rains, and sit on the dried grass whenever the sun would come out from behind the clouds and the warriors would call for him.

7
Zoom on Zanzibar

A scooter came racing around the corner. My hand grabbed Miles and yanked him toward me.

'Miles, p-l-e-a-s-e, don't walk in the middle of the road, you'll get run over.'

I was impatient. I was lost. I was thirsty.

There were no proper sidewalks for us to walk on and what passed for sidewalks was just about wide enough for one civilized person, not for a mother and a wild young man. Women covered head to toe in black passed us, their faces covered by veils that revealed little more than their eyes. Those pairs of black eyes would follow Miles and it was easy to imagine the smiles behind their veils. Children were playing chase in the maze of narrow alleyways. A large door elaborately decorated with carved quotations from the Koran opened and the scent of spice and clove oil entered the street and hit our noses. Images of an exotic town, a labyrinth that transfers you back into the times of One Thousand and One Nights. Stone Town. A hot steaming soup of Swahili culture mixed with Arabian religion and architecture and, undoubtedly, a lot of spice.

I didn't spend as much time in this fascinating place as I would have done without Miles. Miles was still too young to do much sightseeing. His legs were too short to walk patiently by my side for any extended length of time. His interest was solely in the undernourished, filthy looking town cats. He longed to pull their tails and pet their backs. I intervened each time with the swiftness of a worried mother. It doesn't take much to envision the kind of germs that those lost creatures generously give to anyone who touches them.

On the roof terrace of the old Africa House Hotel, a then famous travelers' hangout for sundowners, Miles did his best to turn a moment of pleasure into a hassle. I drank the one beer that I bought during the 25 minutes of our stay like medicine. After the first two sips I gulped it down in a hurry. Miles made me edgy. He ran slalom in-between the legs of the tight backpacker crowd that stood around, engaged in the typical travelers' talk.

I managed to speak to a total of two and a half people, travelers from Scandinavia, of which I met many in Eastern Africa. After a conversation that was so short it was almost impolite, I ran around apologizing to about thirty or forty people who wondered why I was sniffing around their knees and feet. I was only trying to find my wild son. Finally I gave up and we left. Stone Town is a romantic place for lovers, an interesting place for historians, but the days become undesirably long when you are with a two-year-old. You cannot wait to go to bed.

I took Miles out of town on the obligatory spice tour. Here in the Gardens of Eden he explored a multi-faceted array of smells and tastes to the joy of the tour guide and the other tourists. He had no apprehension about licking black pepper corns and ginger, peeling cinnamon bark off the tree, sticking cloves in his nostrils, and eating fresh pineapple until the juice was dripping from his T-shirt, elbows and chin. He walked, tasted, touched, waited and listened like an adult.

At the end of the day our guide invited all of us to his home. His wife had prepared a traditional meal for us. Miles was welcomed with open arms by the Muslim family. He ate little of the food, since the many cats that appeared from all corners of the stone house kept him on his toes.

The following day Miles and I traveled even further away from bustling Stone Town, right to the other end of the island, to a small place called Nungwi.

Nungwi: A village, a cliff, and a beach! That's where we spent four weeks filled with mom-son moments. Here Miles made friends with the young and the old, the locals and the tourists.
I know that for the fast paced amongst us, the cram-it-all-in-one-weekend-people, it would have been the most boring holiday of their lives. Swimming in crystal clear shallow waters, dubious boating in overloaded vessels, turtle watching, cutting up mangoes and pineapples, and showering off your sandy bottoms with cold water, nothing else than that for 28 days!

In fact, I overheard several tourists complain after as little time as one week. There was the young German who thought of himself as indispensable to his company. Filled with duty he crossed the island every 48 hours in order to check his email in an air-conditioned Internet café in Stone Town. Another impatient case was the American who would race across the beach on a rented motorcycle. He got arrested. At least he ended up having some action and an exciting story to tell, more than mellow Nungwi would offer to the civilized.

Miles and I didn't violate the law. We didn't get arrested, yet we were deprived of our breakfast without prior warning. I thought the twenty-five-year-old Zanzibari with the goofy smile who always hung out at the resort's restaurant was joking when he told me one morning that from now on breakfast was cancelled. It was the beginning of Ramadan, the month of fasting for Muslims. The owners of the resort were Muslim, and during the time of Ramadan religious belief forbids the faithful from preparing or consuming any food from sunup to sundown. That seemed like an awfully long time to wait for your breakfast.

Nevertheless, I was perplexed about the sudden news. I felt cheated. I had paid for one full month of H&B, hut and breakfast. Admittedly, the amount of money wasn't worth talking or fighting about, but still, it put me in a grumpy mood.

So Miles and I went out in search for a plan B. We didn't have to go far to bump into a less orthodox Muslim who saw it as a great business opportunity to serve food to starving Christians and other non-Islamic humans. His restaurant, a balcony reaching over a cliff onto the sea, turned out to be an idyllic place for our breakfast that became a ceremony we both looked forward to.

We watched the morning divers pop up out of the water. We saw local women and kids standing along the shore with their plastic buckets waiting for the tide to lower. Then they would wade through the shallows parallel to the shore with their heads bent down looking for eatables. Meticulously they collected everything that moved. The sealife they threw in their buckets looked like brown blobs of Play-Doh dipped in mustard. There were dhows to count, the legendary sailboats that used to cross the Indian Ocean with the wind blowing in what looks like a king size bed sheet. And there were persistent monkeys and birds to be chased away by Miles or by mom.

I sacrificed the milk that was meant to go into my coffee and poured it over Miles's cornflakes. Here at the beach milk was a culinary treasure that would require an across-the-island trip to a Stone Town supermarket. Folic acid, calcium, Vitamin D, and a fresh ocean breeze. What more could you wish for your child's healthy development? Every morning we spent at least one hour at the breakfast table - eating, speaking, looking - something that seems difficult to achieve at home.

After several days of staying at the resort I felt I was more than just a paying guest. The treatment that I received from the women and men who run the place was that of a daughter. The men watched me walk into town, and it was clear that they would have interfered had I been exposing too much of my skin. To test my suspicion, one afternoon I pretended to walk into town, although I actually wanted to go to the beach. Collectively the men gestured that I shouldn't visit the village in a bikini top. They were caring people really. They looked after Miles and made sure that he was smiling at all times. They gave him sweets. They never got tired of greeting him with smiles and waving to him.

Miles and I shared one bed, one chair and one table that stood outside under the thatched roof of our deck. We shared the one floor that measured 9 square feet and that was constantly covered by a thin layer of sand. Amazing how a child manages to carry buckets of sticky sand on his skin, behind his ears and in his swimming trunks into the place where he undresses. Even after a shower, grains of sand still fell off his body.

The simplicity of my new lifestyle was extremely soothing, and it made for a better relationship with my son. All my inner tensions had disappeared. Besides the occasional power struggles between a parent and a child, nothing of an unnecessary nature spoiled our togetherness.

'Let's get our beach gear and go.' I yelled for Miles after I finished cleaning our hut.

Miles had been playing with the two cats that lived on the premises. He came running. I took his hand and we wandered to the beach where we would catch a ride on a wooden fisherman's boat that carried about ten people to the neighboring cove. Nungwi beach had no shade, so we spent the day in Kendwas Rocks.

We climbed out off the boat, I put my bag down in the hot sand, and Miles took off. He splashed water at his playmate, a local kid who had a European mother and a local father. He was a cute looking half-caste with mocca frappucino skin and long curly hair. The four-year-old boy would sit with us at his mom's restaurant and we all would eat juicy king fish filets.

If Miles and I had to decide on one dish that we would want to eat for the rest of our lives, it had to be king fish a la Zanzibar. After lunch Miles would take a nap at the beach, exhausted from the heat. When the boat would come to take us back to Nungwi, I usually had to wake him up. Other times, when the tide was low, I walked all the way home, carrying him in a cloth on my back for several miles.

The hostility of the local population toward the influx of tourists who wouldn't respect their Muslim tradition and straddled through their village in beach gear staring into their doorless and windowless coral homes onto their poverty was apparent. Think about busloads of Japanese getting off in your street, peeping through the curtain of your front window taking pictures of you on your sofa picking your toes. How would you feel? However, the eyes of children never seem as threatening, as judging, as comparing as the eyes of adults with their photographic lenses. Miles was a welcome guest in and around their impoverished existences.

The daily game of tag with the local kids soon had its routine. Miles jumped over chicken heads, concrete doorsteps, unfinished white coral walls, piles of damp laundry, buckets of water, elderly people's legs and terrified babies, always in the pursuit of the running legs that belonged to the village youth. It was nice that we didn't have to ring doorbells, we didn't have to share the same language, we didn't need to arrange playtime. Kids came running as soon as they saw *mzungu mtoto*, the white baby. Sometimes I followed, always keeping a respectful distance, never entering their homes. When everyone was exhausted, Miles was brought back to me holding the hand of an older child.

Dinner was another special occasion. Miles attracted travelers from all over the world to our table. Maybe because of his age, people were curious how I managed or maybe because of his smile, his charm, rarely did we sit alone. Goodnight stories were read to him across the table in different languages and with different accents. And that's where for the first time, and little did we know back then that it wouldn't be for the last time, his Daddy-to-be read Dr. Seuss's *Green Eggs and Ham* to him. He read louder than everyone else. He turned the pizza restaurant into an open-air theatre. Heads turned. Mouths stopped chewing on pizza. As a mother I thought Mike was great, funny, wonderful. Miles thought the same. Who cares what the other tourists thought who were forced to listen.

Until this day Mike claims that I had followed him from Arusha to Zanzibar. The one night that I saw Mike on the Arusha campsite I thought he was very attractive and perhaps I would have followed him had I known that he was traveling to Zanzibar. I didn't. It was my destiny that helped out.

Sometimes I would bring Miles's Africa puzzle to the restaurant, a wooden jigsaw puzzle that I had bought at the Maasai market in Nairobi. Its colorful pieces resembled the African countries. The African continent was in one color, without lines or borders. To this day Miles does this puzzle with incredible determination and speed. I bet many travelers that my two-year-old would beat them in completing the puzzle. We timed them, and each time Miles won. Well, can you place Uganda on the African map, or Gabon, within less than three seconds? If you can't, you are the one paying for the drinks tonight! Miles would like a mango juice and I would like an ice-cold Tusker, please.

8

Malaria Ghosts

It was a practical decision that prompted me to smuggle Miles past the Zanzibari immigration officers. His six page fold-out children's passport was filled with stamps and visas and we still had three international borders to cross before we would be home. Avoiding the Zanzibari departure stamp and pushing my short fellow underneath the high counters of immigration was easier than arranging for all the required paperwork to get a new passport issued by the German consulate.

An unsteady boat ride on the hydrofoil Sea Express brought us to mainland Tanzania. Our playful and entertaining time on the spice island Zanzibar, whose name alone makes you want to go there, had come to its end, and in my mind I was already painting the mental picture of flying to the Middle East, our last stopover on this trip.

Both of us were feeling well. We had barefooted Zanzibar's sandy roads and beach bars without becoming acquainted with the jigger, a fly that loves to lay its eggs in the soft skin that surrounds your toenail. Several tourists at Nungwi had caught the jigger. Miles had watched how a local pulled one of those black wormlike things out of a German doctor's foot. It was huge and had to be taken out in one piece.

All that Miles and I needed to do at this point of our trip was to get back to Nairobi on one of those buses that take you halfway through East Africa for $2.50. One of those bus rides where you get what you pay for. Not an unfamiliar ride for us though.

We fought our way through the Dar es Salaam port area that seemed permanently clogged with thieves who disguise themselves as tourist guides, porters and helpers of all sorts. After unloading our luggage at the hotel, we went to buy the bus tickets for our trip to Arusha, where we had to stop over for the night. Triumphantly I emailed all my friends and family to let them know that we had survived East Africa without being stabbed, burnt, eaten alive, drowned or infected.

Yet on the same day that I felt so safe and boasted about it, something ugly came up on the horizon like a thunderstorm after the calm. The horror of this day made sitting in my living room in England and staring at the raindrops on my window the most desirable thing in the world. Without batting an eyelid I would have exchanged idyllic white beaches and indigo skies for any dumpy existence outside of the tropics. The distressing moment of truth came unexpectedly on the very day that I felt so safe.

It was early evening. Miles lay stretched out on the hotel bed, snoring. I was folding T-shirts and sandwiching books between clothes in order to distribute the weight of my backpack evenly. I had already discarded some of my luggage. Most of Miles's T-shirts were so dirty that even the strongest bleach wouldn't be able to clean them, so they went in the trash, too. I had given my sleeping bag to a girl from South Africa who I met on Zanzibar. Michelle drove one of those overlanders that cover all the tourist highlights on the Johannesburg - Nairobi route. For some reason she needed another sleeping bag.

Relieved of almost 30% of our previous luggage, I still hauled an old-fashioned, pretty heavy tent along. I had purchased it secondhand in Nairobi in a fabrics store with a Rent-a-Tent business. The Indian shop owner who ran the business from behind huge rolls of cloth had promised to buy it back off me for a little less than I had paid him in the first place. A cheap deal I couldn't afford to miss out on.

As the evening went on I found a place for everything in my backpack. Next to the pack sat a white plastic bag filled with food for the 14-hour bus ride that awaited us. I had bought cookies, water, soda crackers with cream cheese and four bananas, the typical stuff you can buy in any African grocery store and that doesn't grow mold in the heat.

I had figured it all out in my mind: I would wear the moneybelt around my waist, the backpack on my back, of course, the plastic bag in one hand and my other free hand was the one that managed Miles.

I took a shower and thought about how I enjoyed not having to remove any sand from between my toes. With a towel wrapped around my body, water dripping from my hair, propelled by some motherly instinct, the seventh sense that all mothers have - as my mom always used to say - or maybe purely by some dreaded coincidence, I went into the bedroom and bent over Miles to stroke his head. He looked so sweet and innocent, like all sleeping children: a half naked angel with a suntan. My hand pulled back instantly. His forehead felt like a burning hotplate.

It was then that I experienced the kind of fear you rarely experience in life. A fear that is more substantial than the fear of failure. A fear that only a life and death situation evokes. One of the effects of that fear is an almost compulsive desire to move around in panic. This desire is interrupted by intervals of paralyzing stiffness, with the result that your body doesn't know what to do, run around or freeze.

I knew he had malaria. No medical diagnosis could have been more precise than my intuition. Miles had complained about diarrhea before he went to bed, and now this enormous heat that emanated from his little head, all devilish symptoms of a virus that had occupied my mind in a curious mélange of horror and respect since I had been traveling in Africa.

Malaria affects a minuscule number of tourists, well ... I stared at Miles for a short moment, my heart beating a hundred miles an hour, saying silent prayers. I loved this child more than anything I had ever loved in my life. The backs of my hands wiped a few useless tears out of my face. I put on a random selection of clothes and ran downstairs. With a trembling voice I explained to the hotel owner that my son had malaria and that we needed to get medical attention as quickly as possible. This gentle man, unusually tall for an Indian, who had treated us with such friendliness that I decided to return to his place on our second time in Dar es Salaam, tried his best to calm me down.

'There is a hospital just one block behind the hotel. One of our men will go with you. Don't worry. Now, go and get your child.'

I nodded a voiceless thank you and flew upstairs taking three steps at a time. Although I held Miles in my arms as if he were a fragile antique china vase the fever woke him up. He cried. His face had changed its complexion to such a deep red that it shone through his tan. He was in pain from the raving temperature. Oh, my God. I was so terrified I thought I was losing it.

It must have been around 9 o'clock in the evening when I entered the dark streets. Two African men, whom I had never met before, appeared by my side. We hurried around the corner to the hospital and I explained my situation in *staccato forte* to the lady at the check-in desk. She announced in a monotonous, almost indifferent voice, 'The doctor will come and see you in a while. He isn't actually here at the moment. So, take a seat in the waiting area, please.'

First, I followed her instructions, but as soon as my thighs touched the sterile hospital chair I jumped up with dramatic speed. I wasn't going to wait for anything in this world. For all I knew it could be an hour, two hours or three before this doctor was going to show up. My frightened Western self wasn't equipped with African patience. In fact, the wish to speed things up can be maddening in a country where patience isn't a virtue but a necessity. I ran along the corridor until I was back on the nightly streets.

'Look,' I said to the local men that had followed me without asking questions, 'we need to take a taxi and drive as fast as we can to the best hospital in town. A private, expensive and good hospital.'

Evidently, I didn't care about the cost. I was desperate. My son's life was at stake. The Tanzanians formed a circle around me, by now it was five or six of them, I don't remember exactly. They had no idea where we should go. Of course not. They would have never in their lives set foot in a private hospital, something that only the wealthy in town and foreigners can afford. Why should they know where these hospitals are?

Frustrated by their bewildered expressions and under great emotional pressure I raised my voice in the same way all ignorant tourists eventually begin to shout when incapable of communicating their desires. Rarely does it occur to us that some concepts aren't transferable, and our ways of coping with certain situations aren't necessarily part of the other culture. It felt like I was being put to the test for a few endless moments. Finally I stopped shouting. I shut up. Feeling sorry for my irrational outbreak I listened to their concerned talk that was conducted in Swahili.

One of them flagged down a taxi and consulted with the driver. By happy chance, this man seemed to know of some place. Impetuously, all of us crammed into the one taxi. 10 minutes later we arrived at a small, private hospital. I wanted to kiss the driver on his cheeks, but left it at a pat on his shoulder. He promised to wait.

I was able to see a doctor straight away thanks to the brotherly assistance of my chaperons, my new African family. They dashed back and forth to provide me with the paperwork that I needed to fill in before the consultancy. They took the tightly rolled up notes that were moist from the humidity and the sweat of my hands, and that smelled so sweet of the tropics, to pay my bill. They pushed the change into my hands. And they made sure I entered the correct room where I should wait for the doctor.

There were no other patients in the emergency room and the doctor came immediately. He took Miles's blood. He said I would have to wait a few minutes for the result. Miles was still crying, his head boiling hot, ready to explode. I felt so demoralized. I sank into one of the chairs in the waiting area, a long white corridor, and didn't speak.

My head spun and my brain went on a strange roller coaster ride. It made me think of the one friend who had told everyone that I was the most irresponsible mother she had ever known. She refused to have anything to do with me since she found out that I was taking Miles to Africa. I closed my eyes and saw my neighbors, family and friends with those blank looks on their faces that I was never quite sure how to interpret. I thought of all the parents who keep their toddlers in child safe and germ free homes and compared them with my poor child, who lived in a strange land in a modest hotel room, who preferred fish to candy bars, and who was now in danger of dying from malaria. And it was my fault.

'He grows up like a gypsy, not sure which place to call home.' The malaria ghosts were speaking to me. 'Taking a young child to Africa? You must have been out of your mind. Now you are going to pay for it. You are going to lose him.'

In my thoughts I fell short of passing even the lowest grade for competent motherhood.

It's in the most desperate moments in life when miracles happen that strengthen our belief in the good of humanity.

Here I sat, surrounded by a group of middle-aged Tanzanian men that I had never seen before in my life. They had just appeared when I needed them. They had things to do, places to go to, families and friends who were waiting for them, yet they had brought their lives to a halt, entirely selflessly, and were there for me; they wanted to help. I was much too thankful for their reassuring presence to question their motives. Was there at all a need to be suspicious only because this would have never happened back home?

One of them continued to help me with Miles, another one ran back and forth with more paperwork to be filled in and stamped, a third one sat next to me invisibly holding my hand. The others sat opposite me waiting silently - just in case they would be needed.

And then it occurred to me that they must have been very patient with this white woman. Malaria is, for many Africans, what a severe flu is for us. I was pretty sure that my Tanzanian brothers had seen much worse. I was a rich mother who had the money to pay for medical care and drugs in a well-equipped hospital.

Sometimes it helps to look at the bigger picture. During my trips to Africa I had met a number of children who had suffered from malaria, but who, after years of living in the same region, developed immunity to the virus. But one of the reasons why malaria is still the number one killer in Africa is because many people live far away from medical care and more often than not can't afford the drugs.

The doctor interrupted my thoughts. He confirmed that Miles had caught malaria and the hospital nurse administered Miles the first shot of chloroquine. A higher dose than you would take on a preventative basis. I was told that his temperature would go down within the next few hours. I had to be back for the second shot 5 o'clock in the morning.

Before I had the chance to show my gratitude to my native chaperons, they had disappeared. The only one still there was the taxi driver. He took me back to the hotel and said he would be waiting for me in front of the hotel shortly before 5 a.m. to give us a ride back to the hospital. Miles had his eyes closed from the exhaustion and medication when I put him to bed. He was breathing calmly. Every ten minutes I checked his temperature. His fever went down rapidly. Staring at the ceiling of the small hotel room I realized that during those difficult moments I hadn't been alone in this city that was so far away from my home.

There was just one last twist to the story. All of a sudden I felt extremely hot in the cool, air-conditioned room. I went to the bathroom and spent some time dealing with severe stomach cramps. Was it my turn now? No, please! I had to take care of Miles. I couldn't possibly deal with malaria!

When we returned to the hospital for his second shot and to pick up his medication for the next three days, the doctor and I talked about my suspicion. He told me that my blood couldn't be tested right now because the guy who worked in the laboratory had gone home. Nevertheless, he was pretty sure that I had malaria, too and, therefore, he gave me a whole bunch of pills to swallow. I started off swallowing them religiously for two days, the rest I threw away.

Miles, the little jack-in-the-box, the traveling ironman, was back on his feet within 24 hours. We left Dar es Salaam a day later than planned and he slept, drowsy from the medication, for most of the bus journey. However, until this day I couldn't tell you if I ever had malaria or not.

9

Bahrain
Why don't you Stay, ay, ay?

Airports and hospitals have in common that they are safe and
dirt-free places for children and hassle-free places for traveling
moms. A strange thought? Or perhaps not so strange depend-
ing on the circumstances you are in. I know what you are
thinking. A public place such as an airport, where thousands of
passengers pass through in one day, or a hospital, where
billions of germs are carried in and out by sick patients, can't
possibly be considered orderly and clean. I agree, but what if
you have been spending the last few weeks in countries where
a layer of dust on your skin is constant, and where people drive
their cars as if possessed by an evil spirit. And where just a few
minutes of play on the ground covers your child's hand with
such a thick coat of black dirt that he could have been on any
airport floor on his hands and knees for as long as you like and
he wouldn't be as filthy.

Believe me, when leaving the big city streets, especially, although not exclusively, in poorer countries and entering an airport, the place feels sterilized and organized. You can run after your restless children without having to fear that somebody will steal your luggage. Remember, you have checked it in before you sat down.

And hospitals? Hmm, yes. Quite rightly. Why on earth would you visit a hospital on your vacation unless you were sick? Sometimes hospitals might be your only choice if you want to cool off and escape the noisy outdoors.

'I'm looking forward to seeing you, finally. It's been such a long time. Call me from the airport, when you get there. We'll have a fabulous time…Lots of love, Ahmed.'

Once more my eyes skipped over the first few lines of his email. It promised a two-week luxury break in Bahrain in his grand villa with, of course, a swimming pool. Much too tempting to refuse, even though I knew that I wouldn't have the cash to survive in expensive Bahrain for very long. Bahrain, a playground for wealthy Saudi Arabians, is an island off the Saudi Arabian shore. A causeway leaves its capital city Manama (Sleeping Place) and reaches the Saudi city of Khobar, connecting Bahrain with mainland Saudi Arabia.

Servants bringing me breakfast, lunch and dinner, doing my laundry… I dreamed on. Why not live the life of the wealthy for a few days? And maybe I could go on a job hunt at my own leisure, just to see what would happen. After all, I had no job to go back to and wouldn't mind teaching in the Middle East for a year or two.

I'm sure Miles would appreciate a bathroom decorated with expensive tiles, as opposed to gray concrete flooring. Just kidding. It is more likely that for him Bahrain would merely be another place.

Two months had passed since I had received Ahmed's invitation. Today we were leaving Nairobi.

'Your luggage will be checked through to Bahrain. You have a two-hour stopover in Abu Dhabi,' explained the ground staff at the check-in counter.

Relieved of my luggage two hours before departure, I sat down in the clean and cool airport hall and tried to get my thoughts back together. This last day in Nairobi had robbed me of my well stocked up energies. Early that morning I did some last minute souvenir shopping in downtown Nairobi. Bad choice. I nearly got mugged. But by lucky chance, the elastic band of my money belt withstood the violent pull. I shouted. I don't remember what I shouted, but I shouted loud. Not that in a city that is as noisy as you imagine any African capital would be would I actually be heard, let alone get some attention. But the big, grabby bandit's claw did let go, and money, passports and plane tickets bounced back on my stomach. Without further ado I grabbed Miles and stumbled into the next taxi that happened to approach us. My initial intention was just to get off the streets. Then I changed my mind.

'To the Aga Khan hospital, please,' I said.

It seemed like a good idea at the time. What else was there to do? We had some time to kill. Once you check out of your hotel, that's it. Our belongings were still sitting behind the reception desk, but we couldn't possibly sit there as well for the next six hours.

So, the huge, privately run Aga Khan hospital in Nairobi seemed like a convenient alternative. It features a courtyard with water fountain in the center and a play area for children, clean restrooms with toilet paper, and, above all, peace and quiet. And no thieves.

Once at the hospital I decided to kill two birds with one stone, and I had Miles's blood checked by an African medic who I was convinced must know more about local parasites than the majority of doctors in the West. The blood test showed that my little travel companion was doing fine, and I would leave East Africa with an appeased conscious.

In the early evening hours we made it to the airport. While I sat and watched Miles play with a fluffy florescent worm on a silky string, I was suddenly overcome with excitement in anticipation of our final part of the trip. I was truly looking forward to Bahrain, a place upon which I had never set foot before. I was also very excited to see my friend Ahmed again after so many years. Ahmed is one of the best people that I have ever met in my life, and he had been one of my closest friends at university. The fond memories that I cherish about the time that we spent together include my visits to his dorm at 4 in the morning. My selfish knocking at his room door would wake him. Dressed in a bathrobe he would agree to sit with me in the communal kitchen and try to sort out my disastrous love life. I sobbed all the way through our conversation. He tried with admirable patience to make me reason and listen to his caring advice. My memories include discussions about world affairs, a trip to the Berlin wall shortly after it opened up to the West, student discos, and drinking flat English lager.

His tolerant, open-minded outlook on things had always surprised me, given that he grew up in one of the strictest Muslim societies. He was born and raised in Saudi Arabia, yet his thoughts and his conduct were in many ways closer to me than those of fellow Europeans. I couldn't wait to catch up on the latest news and to introduce Miles to him. And I was sure he would have some splendid ideas about how to get a job that would set Miles and me up comfortably.

The airport building in Abu Dhabi served as an appetizer of what was going to await us in Bahrain. Futuristic architectural designs mixed with Islamic features dipped into gold and sprinkled with diamonds. The departure hall featured a huge dome-like ceiling, blue and golden decor, and the store windows were overloaded with pearls and shiny jewelry. A cross between Harrods in London, the Alhambra in Granada and a space ship. Magic Arabian nights. But, by Allah, how overwhelming for an airport.

Without exception, the Arabic passengers that waited with us at the gate were male, strutting around dressed in dark designer suits and polished shoes. I began to feel out of place in my ragged backpacker outfit. I wasn't dirty or smelly. I had, of course, showered in the morning. But I wore a black T-shirt that quite obviously had been washed more than just a few times and a pair of khaki hiking pants. And Miles ..., well, how can you keep a toddler clean and well dressed in fashionable clothing when you are backpacking without a washing machine and a box of easy wipes? His trousers showed some stains around the knee area and his face was in desperate need of a wash. It always is. I haven't as yet discovered how to keep my child's appearance as immaculate as other parents do.

Everyone could tell that he had eaten chicken on the flight from Nairobi to Abu Dhabi.

However, I was to feel even more out of place once I arrived in Bahrain. Neither the airport was posher nor the people dressed as glamorous, but it was midnight when we arrived, and I was wandering around the arrival and departure halls in search of an ATM, pushing a trolley with a crying toddler seated on the summit of our mountain of luggage. I was unveiled, displaying my long blond hair. I was a woman on her own, without a husband, male chaperon, male friend or relative by my side. I painted an obscure picture for those Middle Eastern men who stared at me with their dark eyes unconcealed. I was glad to have Miles with me. At least Miles proved that I was a mother and not a single woman on her own in public in the middle of the night, slash prostitute.

It was hard to ignore the staring eyeballs around me. I tried to concentrate on the ATM screen in front of me. I was tired and nervous. Most of the men were covered in white outfits that looked like bed sheets to me, flung over their shoulders and draped around their heads, leaving just a small opening for their face. Not being used to it, it made me feel uncomfortable.

I was about to withdraw a small amount of Bahraini dinar in order to make a phone call, but I had no idea about the current exchange rate, nor could I read Arabic letters. Without thinking properly I pressed the upper left button. Anywhere in the world this would have worked in my favor, except in those countries where people read from the right to the left. Consequently I withdrew an undesired large stack of Bahraini cash in order to buy nothing but a phone card.

Miles was whiny. Maybe he needed to go to the restrooms to have his diaper changed. 'Come on Miles, you can do it. Ignore your needs.' I'm talking to myself here. 'Let me make this one phone call to Ahmed. It'll be really quick and then we are out of here and we'll have plenty of time to clean you up.'

At the desk of a rent-a-car office that was still open at this time of the night I enquired, where I could buy a phone card. Several local men turned to us to give me directions. Their looks followed me as I walked off.

I took the elevator to the next floor. Eventually I found the tiny cafeteria that they had talked about that was open at 1 in the morning. It sold phone cards. After the successful purchase of the card I still hated myself for agreeing with Ahmed to call him from the airport rather than meeting him at an agreed time. I wasn't equipped with a mobile phone that would work anywhere in the world. And besides, Miles cried.

Miles probably wished he could hibernate for the next six months. He was well beyond sleepy and his butt was sore from sitting too long in diapers that needed a change. My calming words quite obviously didn't solve the problem. I was cruel to him. But I thought I was doing the best for us by calling Ahmed and getting him to pick us up as soon as possible. In addition, I was stressed out and so chose to ignore Miles's apparent needs for the time being.

There were four people waiting in line for the phone. I stood around, waited and gave a desperate impression. A giant sheikh clothed in white curtains approached me in a fatherly manner.

'Where is your husband?' he asked in perfect English.

'He is at home in Europe,' I lied.

The sheikh raised his eyebrows in disbelief. He must have watched us for a while just like everyone else in the arrivals hall. I told him why I had come to Bahrain and why I waited to use the phone. So he waited with us, not directly standing next to me, but near enough.

Miles cried and cried, but I didn't want to lose my spot in the line and I was too anxious to ask the sheikh to do us a favor and stand in line until we come back from the restrooms. Finally, it was my turn.

'Hi, Ahmed. It's me, Stefanie. We have arrived in Manama.'

'You, in Bahrain? What is today's date? I mean, did you say you were coming today?' Ahmed's voice sounded confused. 'I'm in Saudi Arabia. My parents are sick. I was called out here yesterday. It's an emergency. Maybe I'll get to Bahrain in a few days. But, look, don't worry. Call this friend of mine. He has the keys to my house. I will arrange everything else over the phone with my servants. They will look after you two. You will enjoy yourself.'

I will what? Enjoy myself? I was in total shock. Without saying a further word, my throat dry, I noted down his friend's phone number. Then I called this man only to listen to the taped voice of an answering machine that spoke to me in Arabic.

Since the answering machine was not going to pick me up from the airport, I seriously needed to think about our sleeping arrangements. For a moment I stood motionless, staring at my crying boy.

'Oh, Miles. What are we going to do now?' I asked myself more than I asked him.

Hotel, bed and some rest. Tomorrow my head would be clearer. A shadow distracted me. It was the fatherly sheikh. He was still hovering around us. Why wasn't he going away? What did he want? I wasn't in the mood for dealing with him.

I was mad at Ahmed, and at the same time I wasn't. I knew he hadn't done this on purpose. He had forgotten about my arrival. Nevertheless, I felt like pulling the phone cord out of the payphone. Then the soft voice of the giant sheikh addressed me.

'Will your friend come soon?'

I was surprised that he asked me such a question, since I could swear he eavesdropped into my calls.

'No. He is in Saudi Arabia.' It was none of his business anyway, I thought.

'He will come. Just wait.'

Did he not understand what I had just said?

'No. He won't come. He is in Riyadh, SAUDI ARABIA. But never mind.' I shrugged my shoulders. Then I tried to shake him off and wandered with my trolley load around a column. He followed.

'Lady. You wait a while and he will come. He is your friend.'

What was wrong with the guy?

'No.' I shook my head. 'I want to get a taxi now and find a hotel room.'

For the first time I looked up into the face of this gentle giant. He had beautiful features, deep brown eyes, a slightly curved nose and tanned, leathery skin. He must have looked stunning as a young man. I smiled at him. He didn't smile back. He was concerned. Maybe he didn't want to let me leave the airport and go off somewhere into the darkness of the night: a mom by herself with a small child.

He escorted us to the taxi stand, spoke to the taxi driver of the first taxi in line, opened the door for me and helped load my luggage into the car.

Exhausted, I sank into the bordeaux leather seats of the Manama taxi. All taxi seats in tropical and subtropical countries seem to be bordeaux. The Arafat look-alike who sat behind the steering wheel turned his head to me and asked me where I wanted to go.

'To the cheapest hotel in town, please,' I said with confidence, and then I closed my eyes, rubbing the back of my sobbing son. Oh, my Lord. His diaper held more than it was designed for. I smelled the evidence. I should have gone to the restrooms with him, but my mind had been so clouded in the last few minutes. After all, I didn't have sufficient funds to survive for more than three days in this expensive city. I stared out of the window into the darkness. I recognized the silhouettes and lights of a wealthy and hypermodern city. Manama. What a funny sounding name for a capital city.

'Here we are.'

I got out of the taxi but told the driver to hang on. With Miles in my arms, I entered the hotel hopefully. The night clerk at the front desk announced, '180 American dollar for one night.' 'Yes, madam, a single room.'

It was probably past 1 a.m., so not even that much night left. $180 seemed outrageous, impossible.

'Thank you.' I stumbled out of the door and ran across the street to the taxi.

'Please, can you find us a very, very cheap hotel?' I asked. 'This one was too expensive.'

The taxi driver nodded and continued the tour.

Ten minutes later I found myself standing at the front desk of a miniature palace, chandeliers dangling dangerously low over my head, this time the taxi driver by my side.

'It's $150 the night, my lady.'

I swallowed. I was frustrated with the taxi driver and the entire situation. I turned around and exited the hotel. Back in the taxi I had a go at the driver.

'Listen. I want to stay in a dump. In a bare room with just a mattress on the floor, with fleas in it, no bathroom, a toilet on the corridor. Please, let's go to the cheapest place in Manama.'

I was impolite now and rude, because I felt so helpless. Did Arafat or Mohammed or whatever his name was not understand me, or did these places not exist in this weekend Mecca for Saudi Arabians? Or maybe the problem was that he just couldn't imagine that a woman without male company, a mother, would want to stay in a simple place. Whatever the reason, we spent about thirty more minutes going to four more places with the same results. The prices were astronomical.

Mohammed stayed quiet. He didn't complain about my pickiness and he didn't get annoyed, he just kept on driving.

Perhaps it was the incessant crying of a child in diapers filled with pooh, or perhaps it was my sudden silence, but something made this polite middle-aged man turn to us and explain, as if to apologize, 'All other hotels that I know of are full with weekenders from Saudi Arabia.'

Yes, the problem was apparent. Bahrain, much more liberal than its Gulf neighbors, where women may go out unveiled and may even drive cars, offers freedom and bars to Muslims from all over Arabia.

'I can find you a hotel Monday night,' the sheikh driver said just to say something.

Monday night? He must be kidding? And tonight we would camp in the streets? For the third time he circled around the city center. Tears shot into my eyes. I felt so forlorn, so foreign and so alien. Come on. Pull yourself together, I thought to myself. I had to find a solution to this unbearable situation. I couldn't just sit in this taxi all night, even though it seemed the only choice I had.

My mind rotated for a while. I felt claustrophobic. I always feel that way when fate seems to take control of me. In those moments I tend to do something irrational, crazy, with the sole purpose of altering the coordinates of the situation that keep me imprisoned.

As a solo woman traveler I would have slept at the airport on top of my luggage. With Miles I had to be more creative. My brain ticked faster and faster. Earlier on at the Manama airport when I was waiting for the phone I had noticed a flight from Germany that came in around midnight. And if I remembered right from studying my onward flight ticket to Frankfurt, my plane was scheduled to leave in exactly two weeks from tonight. I hoped the flight that had come in would return to Germany the same night, in other words now.

'To the airport, please,' I said with a trembling voice.

Mohammed didn't react. Did he not hear me?

'Back to the airport, please.' I raised my urging voice.

I had to end this nightmare on four wheels. Still no reaction from the front seat. Had he fallen asleep? Impossible with Miles crying.

'TO THE...' before I finished my sentence his head turned in slow motion.

'But, but, dooo, dooo, don't you like my country?'

He continued asking me this question for the remaining time that we spent together. A difficult question to answer after an almost two-hour, not entirely problem free, sightseeing tour in grand circles around and around and then straight across Manama in the darkness, don't you think?

We had changed directions. I saw the lights of the airport. Then everything happened fast. Over-tipped, Mohammed left perplexed. I hauled my luggage trolley into the departure hall and stopped two inches short of the shiny shoes of the next best Muslim that I came across and whistled, 'Watch my bags, please. I'll be back in a second.'

In the restroom I relieved my two-year-old of his grief. Immediately he stopped crying. I hurried back to Mr. Surprised, who had herded my luggage with a watchful eye. I gave him a handful of notes from my fat bundle of Bahraini dinar. I had no time to watch the reaction on his face. Completely out of breath I reached the check–in counter.

'The flight to Germany.' I yelled, not even bothering with forming an intelligent question.

'Yes, madam,' the Arab flight attendant responded. 'Aren't you a little late? The flight is leaving within the next few minutes.'

'I have to get on it.' I tried to sound truly desperate, and probably did. 'I have a ticket for in two weeks, but my son is very ill and I have to fly today.'

To my surprise I didn't have to break out in tears or throw myself on the floor. I didn't even have to say one more word. Within seconds, the attendant checked the availability of seats. He spoke into his walkie-talkie, and then he looked at me with a smile and asked calmly, 'Madam, are you ready to run?'

Not awaiting an answer, flight attendants one, two, and three appeared from behind the counter. They jumped beside me. One pushed my trolley, the other one took my hand luggage. I nodded and ran without protest. Miles sat on my hips. The third guy shouted orders into my ears. 'Passports, your visa, flight tickets. Passports again!'

I looked at the Arab who was running in front of me with my carry-ons. Nappies were sticking out of one of the bags, Miles's furry tiger out of the other. Bearded serious sheikhs running full speed with bags full of baby items. It looked hilarious. I had to laugh so hard I nearly tripped.

And before I even knew it, I sat in the last row of a plane with the final destination Frankfurt. A snoring sound beside me told me that my son had fallen asleep instantly. I was told to fasten our seat belts, so I lifted Miles onto my lap. We were ready for take-off.

Ironically, a mother receives exceptional and preferential treatment in a part of the world where men rule. After all, a mother is still a woman.

One last word I have to add. It's an apology for underestimating the quality of my friendship with Ahmed. Worried like only a brother would be, he had somehow managed to get in contact with his friend in Bahrain and he had ordered him to the airport. His friend then told him that he had checked the entire airport building but had been unable to find me. Ahmed then called my mother in Germany to find out where I could possibly be, five minutes after I had arrived at her home.

10

Thailand

A Distant Country

A whipping charge of adrenaline shot through my body. My hands chopped through the air gesturing despair, urgency, emergency. I was unable to talk. I turned around and left my husband and son standing in the middle of a white and gray airport corridor and ran in the reverse direction, inevitably bumping into people. The reason for my sudden change of direction was that my moneybelt with cash, credit card and passport were still on the plane.

'I can't believe that I have ruined this trip for all of us.' It hit my brain with an unpleasant bang.

This will be the end of the world trip, the trip I had been looking forward to for months and had saved up for. It had been the dream of my life.

All my endeavors to get back onto the plane that had brought us from Cologne to London failed. A NO ENTRY sign stood in my way and denied access to the interior of the plane. So what if the plane took off before I was able to retrieve my valuables? Nobody would care. Planes stick to their schedules.

My body ran mindlessly along corridors. My eyes were searching for an information desk. Heathrow Airport certainly wasn't a small grass field anymore, like in the old days. It is the world's busiest international airport, with 64 million passengers passing through long and indistinguishable corridors and lobbies every year. And these corridors seemed to be growing magically with the urgency of my situation.

Eventually I came to a huge hall congested with people and their luggage trolleys. At the far right there was a large information desk with eight lines of people that stretched out like the arms of an octopus. I'm sure that all of those people's concerns and questions were just as important as mine, but I lacked the patience and politeness to wait. I barged in front of the first person in the line closest to me.

I half gasped, half barked at the young man in uniform, 'Excuse me. I left my passport and credit card on the plane. Can you do something about this right now? It's urgent! The plane might take off any second and I need my passport.'

I could tell he wasn't happy with me jumping the line, but, being English, he, in contrast to me, was polite enough to deal with my inappropriate conduct. He immediately established contact with the cleaning crew on the plane. He then asked me to wait for what seemed like forever, but what totaled just about ten minutes. I hopped from my right foot onto my left like a teenybopper at a rock concert.

If I don't at least get my passport back, we would have to go to the German Consulate and spend the first six or seven weeks of our world trip in London. By the end of those weeks we would be bankrupt, and my husband Mike would possibly file for divorce. Why would anyone want to be married to such a mindless traveler like me?

I swear to God, things like this never used to happen to me, but once you have a child and a husband you lose your memory.

'Silly mom,' Miles would say if he were with me right now. He would roll his eyes and shake his head dramatically. In school he might forget his sweater, but when it came to traveling he had always kept a good eye on our belongings, even at the age of two. I remember how he used to get mad at people in Africa who merely offered to carry my luggage, as he must have thought they wanted to run off with it. And how on several occasions he had picked things up that I was about to leave behind. He was travelwise like that. He simply puts me to shame.

Admittedly, I had been far too relaxed that day, because for the first time I was actually traveling with another adult. Someone I could lean on. However, I have no idea why my subconscious mind assumed that Mike would be the one looking after MY valuables. A string bean of an officer interrupted my thoughts. He held the retrieved moneybelt in my face.

'Check if everything is still in there,' he ordered.

I opened the zips of the moneybelt, stuck my fingers in it and nodded.

'Yes, yes, yes. Thank you.'

I forgot to tip the guy. My knees were shaking as I tried to find my way back to the staircase where I had left Miles and Mike behind. Hopefully, they would still be standing there.

Of course they were. Where else would they go? Mike didn't ask any questions. He didn't need to. He knew what had happened. He grabbed Miles, who was busy trying to trip up any fast-walking passengers that came his way, Children! Since we had almost 10 hours to kill, we left the airport and dove into the London city crowd. We ate Mexican food, drank Margaritas and Root Beer in 20 minute intervals, and let the diverse mass of people that passed by the restaurant window take our minds off the slow passage of time.

Miles had always enjoyed traveling on a plane. So much so that his eyes sparkled each time he pressed the button to call the flight attendant. On the British Airways flight to Bangkok, he called the attendant barely two seconds after he sat down. It must be a rewarding experience for any four-year-old to be in total control of an adult. And, indeed, he had learned very quickly that flight attendants would bring him a drink even before everyone else had boarded. He also knew that 20 minutes into the flight he would be honored with a travel game and a few crayons, a coloring book and a second drink and peanuts. He had the choice of apple juice, orange juice, water or Coke, not just water or milk, like at home. And, although the food didn't taste all that great, the unwrapping of it was exciting enough, as was the way it came squeezed into the little compartments of a plastic tray. I could tell that he wished I would serve his dinners on one of those things.

Not long ago I read an article in the Condé Nast Traveler magazine that talked about the nightmares of taking a toddler on vacation. The author, a mother of a wild child, was appalled that the car seat wouldn't fit into the plane seat and that she had to gate-check it with the result that her toddler couldn't be strapped in properly and was jumping up and down during the entire flight.

There, again, I am blessed with a child that neither at the age of one-and-a-half, nor two nor four would go nuts in public and pester everyone around him. Flying, to Miles, is something we would do every once in a while, an activity like going to the swimming pool or like watching a soccer match. There was no reason to misbehave, especially since he enjoyed flying.

Quite ironically, I am the one in the family who hates flying. Enigmatically, each time I fly, the seat feels more uncomfortable than the last time I traveled. And, although airline slogans promise comfort and luxury on board their carriers, my legs cramp up, my neck stiffens and the longest I can sleep is the few minutes that it takes until my head drops forward and my mouth opens. Out of reflex I immediately fling my head back up and open my eyes. Then I wish I was four and I had short legs. I could curl up on my seat and sleep like a cat.

Finally, our plane arrived at Bangkok International Airport. Miles's travel mascot, a furry tiger, flew up into the air and landed on the laps of an elderly couple that sat a few rows behind us. Everyone laughed about the flying cat. I suspected it was the relief that we had arrived safely mixed in with the strange effects of low cabin pressure that made everyone display an awkward sense of humor rather than my son's wild throw. The couple that had been bombarded with the stuffed animal, however, ignored the tiger. Instead they praised Miles for having slept so well during all the hours that we had been in the air. Oh, yes, indeed, he had slept so well, hadn't he? Dear me, they really rubbed it into my fatigued face.

In April, the difference in temperature between an air-conditioned airport and the streets of Bangkok amounts to a health hazard. We began to sweat as soon as the automatic glass doors opened. While we sat on a low bench waiting for the bus that would take us to the city center, sweat pearls were dripping from Miles's ears, hair and neck. I had to watch out for him to make sure that his small body got plenty of electrolytes. To my dismay, our daypacks were empty. Cheerfully, and without thinking ahead, we had eaten all the snacks and drank all the liquids. Should I run back inside the airport and see if I can find some bottled water? A difficult decision to make because there was the bus. According to my map the bus ride to the cute little guesthouse that we had selected would only be about 20 or 30 minutes long. So we hopped on the bus. Unfortunately, Bangkok turned out to be busier, hotter and more crowded than expected. In fact, it felt as if on this particular afternoon the city's 10 million inhabitants had all left their homes to go somewhere. And the supposedly 20-minute bus ride turned into a half-day excursion. Fresh off the plane we stood squashed between other travelers in the back of the bus. The lack of air-conditioning in the bus made the inside of the overcrowded vehicle about 10 degrees hotter than the outside. The vehicle was an oven. Our bodies rocked back and forth with the constant stop and go of the traffic. Miles was leaning against our backpacks, still standing upright. He was quiet.

I stared out of the window and was impressed by the mirror-glassed skyscrapers that caught the reflections of the corroded roofs of poor peoples' dwellings, the crowns of tropical trees and the silver and golden roofs of Buddhist temples that portrayed to me images of scaly, shiny, gigantic fish. These were my first glimpses of an immense city that grows and grows at mind-numbing speed.

As the bus ride wore on I eavesdropped on the conversation between two young Spanish girls. One of them had already spent several months in Thailand. With her throaty voice she explained to the newcomer, whom she had picked up from the airport, everything you possibly want to know about Thailand and about the bizarre group of tourists that she hung out with. She spoke incredibly fast. I was captured by her gossip and the clichés with which she embroidered her talk when I suddenly saw the skin around Miles's mouth turn pale and bloodless. His blood pressure was sinking rapidly and his eyes stared at me saucer shaped. No wonder he felt faint, as the other passengers were struggling to suck in the last few molecules of oxygen left on the bus. The fact that he was hot-dogged between two Thais saved him from falling onto the ground.

I panicked. A seat. Where? How? He needed to sit down. As a last resort I pushed my boy on someone's lap in order to save him from passing out. There wasn't much else that I could do now. Miles was always so amazingly calm when indeed he really suffered. Finally, the people around us started to react to the situation. A Thai woman gave Miles a drink. Somebody else offered him a seat. Unfortunately, Miles had to be brave for quite some time longer. We were still stuck in traffic in a city with a rush hour that makes getting around slower than on elephants 200 years ago. I gave him reassuring rubs over his back and he recovered a little. So early into the trip and we were already pushing his boundaries.

When we got off the bus Miles was thrown into the back of a tuk-tuk. Tuk-tuks, or motorized tricycles, are the kind of transport that everyone who is in a hurry uses. They zigzag around cars, buses and anything else that moves on the streets. The tuk-tuk drivers take you from A to B in record time. Behind the driver are seats for four people facing each other on two short benches mounted in a cubicle. The space was quickly filled with our three backpacks and us two adults. Miles sat half on top, half in-between the luggage, taking joy in riding in the open air. Mysteriously, he had morphed from being a worn out little boy into an energized kiddo. His cheeks turned rosy and he looked at the bewildering variety of samples of Asian life that flew by until he discovered the white cloth that the driver wore over his nose in a dentist-like fashion. It was the driver's face and his protective scarf against the pollution that from then on received Miles's devout attention. It is phenomenal how children can forget thirst and faint with an almost natural ease the moment they are distracted.

For myself, I thought that any roller coaster ride at a state fair was much safer than a tuk-tuk ride, and not as bad for your lungs than the hot, polluted Bangkok air that sticks to your skin, thick and black, as you try to cut through it. Not that I would be inclined to swap the precious Bangkok experience with an afternoon at the fair. After all, Bangkok was a real place with real people.

Dusk was on its way. The tuk-tuk slowed down after entering a part of the city with narrow streets, small street cafes, and poorer people. We swerved off the street onto the pavement and came to an abrupt halt. The driver pointed to a slim, dark alleyway across the street.

This must be it. I jumped off the wagon and walked along rusty tin walls into the darkness, all of a sudden not so sure if the driver had understood where we wanted to go. I stumbled over garbage until I came to a large wooden door. It was locked and I didn't see a doorbell. I was about to bang against the door to make myself noticed when my eyes caught sight of the unconventional doorbell above my head: a string that dangled down to be pulled by whoever would actually spot it in the dark.

A fragile old lady opened the door. I asked for a double room in English. She understood, and she nodded. Nevertheless, she looked astonished when I didn't enter but pointed to the street and galloped back through the alleyway to get Mike and Miles. Mike followed me with a dubious look on his face that changed into a smile upon stepping into a dimly lit, humid courtyard decorated with tropical plants and surrounded by fine structures made from teakwood. Hammocks hung from large beams. A tranquil oasis amid a hectic city. The Thai owner led us across the courtyard to a large bedroom that was accessible through an outside door. We were ready to fall through the door onto the beds. But there was no chance in hell that we could just do that. The Thai lady stood in the doorway like a prison warden on patrol.

'Shoes off!' she scolded us in Thai.

Not that I understand the language, but I understand gesture and tone of voice. Obediently, we bent down to follow her orders. Barefooted we investigated the room-for-the-night and found it acceptable, especially the king size bed that the three of us were going to share. The polished wooden floors cooled our sweaty feet. During the time that we spent in Thailand, Miles got to practice and very much enjoy the Thai etiquette of taking your shoes off before entering a building. Like most children, he preferred to live barefooted anyway.

Besides the bed and the dresser there wasn't much else in the room, but when our backpacks finally towered in the corners the room was full. On my bare feet I tiptoed through the dark house trying to find the bathroom for Miles. I felt an indiscriminating relief of the sort that I always feel at the end of a long travel day. The weight is off my shoulders.

It had been a trip of extraordinary length for a four-year-old. I was well aware that Miles needed his sleep before the notion of having to travel with his parents would amount to a disincentive for him. But there were still a few situations our minds and bodies had to deal with before they could rest. Our barefooted host waited for us in the hallway. Taking advantage of the unusual opportunity to have a foreign toddler in her house, she seemed eager to show us everything she owned that very night. I was far too worn out to make conversation. The *Fata Morgana* of my bed danced in front of my eyes. Nevertheless, I was polite enough to follow her. I didn't want to offend her a second time.

She was delighted with Miles's happy smile. She pulled him in front of one of her treasures, a dragon, an impressive piece of Asian art. Miles called it a monster. In the hope that she overheard his remark I corrected him in a teacher like fashion.

'What a beautiful d-r-a-g-o-n. Miles, look. A dragon.' I said.

Miles ignored me and insisted on the monster, and we probably did insult her a second time. She took it well, but I guess here in Asia, showing your real emotions is a taboo, so you never know. With a gentle smile she turned around in order to show us the chicken. Miles dropped the monster-thing and followed her to see the feathered animals of the house. How come there was still so much energy left in his little body? We looked everywhere, under the stools and the table. I didn't see any chicken and I also noticed the disappointment on Miles's face. The woman carried on in Thai, dropping the word chicken here and there. I gave up. But then it dawned on me that she must have meant KITCHEN. Her strong accent just made it sound like chicken. Oh, well. We needed a rest.

I excused us and said to Miles, 'Let's go to sleep. Tomorrow we'll look for the chicken. They are already asleep somewhere.'

Mike opened the room door and surprised us with his clean look. Not a person who wastes time, he had unpacked what we needed for tonight and tomorrow. He had washed and was dressed to go out. Then it struck me that we hadn't eaten anything for hours. I grabbed my towel to shower with Miles.

'There is no more running water,' Mike pointed out as if it wasn't a big deal. 'Some backpackers showered before us and they must have used up all the water. I had the last few drops.'

'Don't worry. Let's just go and grab something to eat and drink,' he added. 'We also need to get bus tickets for tomorrow. I want to get out of this crazy city as quickly as possible.'

We stuck Miles in a high-tech Baby Björn for toddlers, one of those that you carry on your back like a backpack. I hoped Miles would fall asleep on his Dad's back, but it didn't happen due to over-stimulation. The lights and action of this bustling city kept him awake.

Our guesthouse was located near Koh San Road, the famous backpacker's haven that offers cheap and reliable food, clothes, souvenirs, videos and entertainment for young tourists. It was early evening. Koh San Road was filled with travelers, tourists, Thai transvestites, night market hawkers, jugglers, and business was thriving. Some were cooking on the sidewalk. We ploughed through the crowd of nightly visitors and stumbled around Thais vending silver rings and bracelets, T-shirts with Bob Marley, Che Guevara, and September 11th prints.

Of course, Miles didn't close his eyes. I wished his eyelids were shutters that I could have pulled down, but children have a mind of their own. On day one of our trip, which in theory had already turned into day two, considering the hours that we had been awake and on the road, Miles decided to stay up until we would all go to bed together. It surprised me. Usually he is not at all like that. Comes his bedtime, he falls asleep regardless of where we are. So we hurried to eat some hot steamed stir fried noodles, jugged down a few glasses of refreshing pineapple juice, bought our bus tickets to get out of town the next day and took a tuk-tuk back to the guesthouse.

I stretched out under the mosquito net. It felt so wonderful. There was a little light shining in from somewhere, just enough so that I could make out the delicately carved bedposts, the bulky shadows of our luggage and the white mosquito net that fell like a comforting veil over my family.

My husband was still turning from one side to the other. I knew it was far too hot for him to get to sleep easily. My son's feet reached up to my waist, his head rested next to my feet. He slept, finally, after having completed a marathon of travel and observation.

All at once I heard a clapping of metal pots. It must have been something like ten or eleven o'clock. I wondered who would still be cooking at this time of the night. I was wide-awake, although exhausted. But I was also wired, thrilled by the thought that the great journey had began. I was in Asia for the first time in my life, and the few Bangkok moments since our arrival had already exposed me to a world I hadn't seen before. Snapshots of small and slim people politely pushing through the streets, Buddhist monks in orange walking past, chickens riding on the backs of motorcycles, thousands of people riding rusty bicycles. Everyone seemed incredibly busy.

I closed my eyes. The way that your ears witnessed the people's lives in the apartments above you and next door reminded me of Spain. However, compared with the Spanish, who cultivate obnoxiously loud habits, the Thais seemed quiet. But the separating walls were paper-thin and the window frames had no glass.

I glanced over to the fragile body of my four-year-old boy. He had managed well so far. Little did he know that tomorrow we would spend half the day in an overbooked minivan with ten other travelers and their backpacks cutting through the pre-monsoon heat from Bangkok down to a coastal village called Laem Ngop.

Miles sat on my lap during the entire trip while Mike juggled his heavy backpack on his knees. The Thai solution to the lack of space in the overbooked van was an even distribution of bags and backpacks on people's knees, so that the three too many passengers could be squeezed into the luggage compartment in the back of the van. Miles, Mike and I sat right in front of the air-conditioning. The driver must have put it on freeze. Several times during the trip we were shivering so much we had to ask him to turn it down. He laughed at us in response and shook his head.

From Laem Ngop we caught a ferry to Koh Chang, an island located in a marine park near the Cambodian border. From the ferry dock it was another 40 minutes or so by taxi to the relatively unspoiled Kai Bae Beach. The taxi was a truck with two wooden benches in the back and a tarp-like roof. We rocked from side to side as we went up and down the hilly island road.

Mike and I hadn't considered it a necessity to call the resorts at Kai Bae Beach ahead of time. Without having made reservations we arrived at Kai Bae Beach on a Thai holiday weekend, one week before the Thai's New Year celebrations, and surprise, surprise, every damn hut, every damn little shady spot under the palm trees was occupied by large Thai families, groups of adolescents and their tents.

Miles ate a bowl of noodles at the restaurant where the taxi had dropped us off and Mike kept him company. I paced up and down the beach in both directions without much luck. Even Porn Bungalows was fully booked, a harmless resort that features 20 basic huts and an interesting name. In my despair I took off on a second round, thinking that this would be the perfect task for the Survivor show. Eventually, I accepted an offer from the French owner of some beach bungalows. He suggested that we pitch our tents in his backyard. Out of breath, I told my two men the thrilling news. Tonight we would be camping. Miles looked at me in disbelief. In his eyes we had taken a 2-hour flight to London, a 10-hour flight to Bangkok, a 3-hour bus ride into the city center, a 20-minute tuk-tuk ride to the guesthouse, a 7-hour bus ride the next morning, a 2-hour ferry ride and a 1-hour taxi ride, that's over 24 hours of traveling time plus another 10 hours of waiting time in between, just to end up camping in someone else's garden. Now, what's the point of that? So, the grand tour of the world began to unfold for Miles like an entry from the Guinness Book of Records rather than a chapter out of Peter Pan.

That night, and many times thereafter, I wondered what concept four-year-olds have of the world. What must have been going through Miles's head when we told him we would be going on a world trip? And what was it all about for us as parents? Was it about relaxation, adventure, travel adrenaline, or about the rare commodity of spending time together doing things? Miles's understanding of geography and of what this trip would be about was limited, for obvious reasons. Nevertheless, his imagination wasn't entirely unprepared, since the map of the world is a standard piece of furniture in our living room. It's four times the size of our TV set. It's a political map, with the states of the world featured in different colors. We stare at it all the time, and while we planned our grand voyage in the spring of 2002, the names of several countries would pop up here and there in the many conversations that we enjoyed at the breakfast, lunch and dinner table.

Before we took him to all those places we explained that it would be a long trip. We would fly over the edge on the one side of the map and come around on the other side. Perhaps it all sounded like a game to him, something fun to do over the weekend. Really, I don't know.

Miles, who had lived in Germany, England and Spain, knew where to find these countries on the world map. He was familiar with the shapes of the African countries, he knew where Alaska is, and understood that the blue on the map is

water. The world trip, I was sure, would fill quite a few of the
many voids that he still had in his image of the world. It would
offer him an abundance of associations from which to choose
when hearing the words Thailand or Fiji or World. And it
would provide him with an understanding of the relation
between distance and time.

A week before we took off Miles had filled his backpack
with some of his favorite toys: a personal stereo, his tiger
teddy, a few books and some small games. The remainder of
his toys we gave away. There was no tantrum, no fit, no
screaming involved. It was easy. Very much like a nomad,
Miles was attached only to a few possessions. He was able to
part with most of his treasures without shedding tears. It made
traveling easy for us, because he never said that he missed
something from home. And he certainly never missed his bike.
I suspect we had bought it too early. He was glad to give it to
someone else. He had always sat on it like a giraffe, stiff and
without much enthusiasm to peddle. Thus, he told the little girl
from next door, 'You can have my bicycle, because I am going
around the world.' And when he said 'world', he rolled the 'r',
so that it sounded important.

The pots stopped clapping. Finally, sleep was creeping up on
me. Being here in Bangkok with a young boy seemed like a
piece of cake. (Just don't leave your passport on a plane.) Miles
was pretty much accustomed to the pains and pleasures of
traveling. He had proven himself to be an excellent travel
companion in many situations. And this time we were not
alone. A strong man would be at our side, prepared to lift my
heavy backpack onto bunk beds and to carry Miles when he
got tired walking. Going around the world with two wonderful

men ought to be relaxing, I thought. I would be able to play a little and sleep a lot and share an entire treasure box full of beautiful experiences with them.

But it was not that simple. It never is. And so the question popped up whether it was good for Miles's development to take him out of kindergarten. The fact that we took him away from a stable location and neighborhood friends preoccupied my mind. I was also worried that Mike's ideas about globetrotting with a child would clash with mine. My husband is a fast-paced person who had suggested visiting twice as many countries as we actually did. Another trace of his personality, one I have a love-hate relationship with, is that he distinguishes himself from a Hollywood stuntman only in two aspects: he doesn't get paid for his stunts and he uses no ropes. What would he be up to on this trip that would frighten me, or worse, endanger our lives?

And while I rested on the Bangkok bed without a pillow to support my head, I saw Mike and Miles flying off cliffs and drowning in seas.

11
Not Every Toilet has a Seat

When was the last time that someone showed you the photographs of his recent holiday trip? Not long ago? Do you remember seeing any photos of toilets? Generally, tourists don't take pictures of places of public convenience, although they have their importance to a traveler's daily life. However, there are exceptions to every rule. A handful of people actually do recognize the importance of latrines and take their picture. You find evidence on the Internet. Just type in 'Toilets of the World' and press search. The variety of photos is interesting, to say the least.

More importantly, what becomes apparent from looking at the pictures is that in some cultures 'doing the business' means spending your time sitting comfortably whilst reading a magazine or an entire book. In other cultures 'doing the business' is a mere necessity that can be done quickly with your eyes and nose closed and without having to sit down. Hygiene, quality of plumbing and design more than often depend on the economic means available. In other words, the wealthy sit on gold.

When you travel, your life becomes more public, since the places you visit are mostly public. So you are constantly exposed to different degrees of cleanliness and privacy. When traveling with children you realize that they don't care as much as you do about all that. On our trips, Miles was notorious for opening the toilet door as soon as he was finished, never mind that I might still be busy. He also put his hands everywhere, blissfully investigating the different kinds of handles, buckets, strings and flushes. He would drive me mad, because I couldn't keep up with his speed. I was always too late with my warnings. Don't touch! People sit on it!

The toilet situation in Thailand stands out in my memory for two reasons. Firstly, it was very diverse, and Miles explored as much as of it he could. Secondly, Thailand was the beginning of our world trip and it took me some time to become attuned to the smelly, the unusual and the disgusting. After a couple of weeks I was fine. Miles never cared.

At the end of our long travel day to Kai Bae Beach on the island of Koh Chang, Miles returned to life. The child who had tirelessly listened to the same two tapes over and over again and who had sat with restraint on laps, benches and seats, finally was allowed to run around. And he sure did. Taking advantage of the freedom and of the attention of a group of female Thai teenagers who couldn't get over his cuteness, he darted in and out of his tent. Each time he appeared with a new toy in his hand, and once he had dragged out his toys he continued with bringing out his clothes. The Thai girls cheered him on with their giggles and clapping. In my head I had decided that it was his bedtime, and maybe he sensed my decision. He certainly avoided looking in my direction.

Had it not been for the mosquitoes, you wouldn't have thought that it was approaching 6 o'clock in the evening. It was still unbearably hot. Far too hot to be camping. But, hey, we congratulated ourselves on having met the friendly Frenchman who allowed us to pitch our tents in his garden behind a line of beach cottages. Our setup on the grassy grounds was almost exquisite compared with the sand and gravel everyone else was camping on. And we had space around us. I quickly noticed that the Thais do their collective best to gather tight, socialize in herds and play their guitars, but without turning into European hooligans.

We didn't have to wait long and *Monsieur, le propriétaire* came checking on us. In between the puffs on his cigarette he pointed to a small beige concrete building with two wooden doors and said, 'I will go and get the keys for the bathrooms. I keep them locked. Too many people around this weekend.'

When he returned he asked for a few dollars before he explained the logistics of the place.

'You just need to turn the water on at the outside of the building. You see? Over there, on the right hand side. That makes the shower work.'

Indeed, I was desperate to have a cool shower. I turned the outside switch as directed before I entered one of the bathrooms with Miles and our flashlight - Miles had played until dark and there was no working light in the shower rooms. In the semi-dark I stood perplexed. Both shower and toilet needed some figuring out. There was a square bathtub made from concrete, there was a hole in the ground next to it with a small wall around its back and both sides, there were two plastic bowls on the floor. Hmm. I didn't see a faucet. Maybe I looked in the wrong places. So we just peed in the hole and slept sweaty and dirty, although it struck me as very disagreeable that the last time we took a shower had been in Europe.

I made sure that we stayed in deluxe accommodation for the following ten days. Well, no, the truth is that at Comfortable Resort – the next place along the beach - all huts were fully booked besides a shack in the far right corner of the property. In desperate search for a room with a breeze, after a sleepless night in the stuffy heat of an arctic tent, Mike didn't care anymore. He had gotten up way before breakfast and found this masterpiece of Asian engineering for us to stay in. A quick look at it was enough to know that there are no building codes in Thailand. But Miles and I accepted his choice without discrimination, and happy to be able to unpack our stuff and to lock it up in this crooked structure made from branches and wooden planks.

The first floor stood on stilts some 20 inches off the ground. It consisted of a small bedroom with a mattress and a mosquito net and a wraparound deck that was lopsided. To the right hand side off the deck there was a hut attached to the first floor, also on stilts, with a toilet, a showerhead, and a massive blue bucket that took up most of the space in the bathroom, and a light bulb dangling from the ceiling. Your typical tree house ladder led to the upstairs. The aluminum roof was so low that you could only sit on the mattresses. A mosquito net walled in the mattresses. Other than that, a few bamboo sticks around the nets were the only things that hindered you from falling from the second floor. Mosquito net walls aren't particularly burglar-proof, so we kept all our valuables and backpacks in the downstairs bedroom.

Basic is probably an overstatement rather than an appropriate description. It was the perfect kind of a hideaway in which boys at the age of four love to hang out and play cowboys and indians or pirates. I'm less sure if it was the perfect place for sleeping and living in, but that's what the current lodging situation had decided for us.

Miles seemed pleased with the idea to sleep all by himself in the downstairs room. He tested his soft foam mattress and unpacked his toys on the deck. He is so brave, I thought. At his age I would have never slept in such a tiny and dark room, particularly in an unknown world that seemed to teem with creepy and crawly things. I would have been far too freaked out. Even today my initial enthusiasm for this unique place, surrounded by bamboo, banana trees and a slow running river, was dampened once I discovered that spiders of all sizes hung from the wooden beams.

I took a broom and chased most of them away. I kept a watchful eye on the remaining ones, checking every so often if they had moved. Miles ran up and down the ladder without a care in the world. No arachnophobia, no claustrophobia, no worries. Mike didn't seem to be bothered either. You can just tell when someone grew up in far-flung places. He went into town to buy a hammock, fixed it above the deck of our new home, and that seemed to be all he needed.

I was desperate for a shower, but again I had to wait. We were only allowed to use the water for the shower in the late afternoons. Instead I went for a swim in the ocean, but the water was lukewarm and salty, of course. Not in the slightest refreshing for our sticky bodies.

While I stood on the deck wrapped in one of my sarongs, Miles came running up to me.

'Mama, where is the kitchen?' he asked.

'There is no kitchen, Miles. This isn't our new home. It is just a place to sleep in for a few nights. We'll eat out,' I explained.

I sat down and helped him fish for the toys that had fallen in-between the wooden planks onto the ground.

'We're going to have fun on the beach. Mama and Papa want to go diving. So, we'll go on a few boat rides, too.' I continued my conversation with him. 'Do you like our garden?'

'What do you mean our garden?' He gave me a funny look.

'Well, look at everything around us. Whatever you see will be our garden for the next couple of days, all these wonderful tropical plants.'

I took Miles's hand and we went for a botanical tour through the rainbow repertoire of the Thai flora.

Later that day, when Mike and I relaxed in the resort's bar, I wondered whether Miles would remember the gigantic bamboo next to our crooked little Thai hut. Will he remember when he is ten that Bamboo makes a squeaky sound when it grows? And will he remember that he asked me if his bones make the same sound when he grows?

I pushed my feet against the bar and swung back on the swing that replaced the bar stools. For the first time I had the feeling that I had truly arrived in Thailand. Rural Thailand. No more bus-ing or taxi riding for the next few weeks. We had found quite a unique looking place to stay, a resort run by friendly Asians. Miles seemed involved in running around with a stick, meeting cats and dogs and playing on the deck, by now more accustomed to the elevated temperatures. And I had finally taken my long desired shower under weird circumstances, but what the heck, I was clean and enjoyed a Thai beer.

A young Chinese guy ran the resort. He was the designated customer relation guy because his English was very good and he enjoyed talking to people more than the average quiet Thai. Shortly after I had informed him on that first afternoon at the Comfortable Resort that my family and I would be taking showers, he came running down the path that led from the main house to our spooky vacation rental.

'I am so sorry, but we are short of water. You have to use the bucket shower for the next two days. The big blue bucket in your bathroom is filled with water, about four gallons or more. It should last you quite a while. If you run out of water let me know. I'll come and fill your bucket again tomorrow.'

He smiled, bowed slightly, turned around and galloped away like a young deer. I guess the situation wasn't unusual for him. And for a $7 per night two-bedroom house you can't really complain.

We began the intimate showering ceremony by squeezing our naked bodies into the tiny bathroom shack. There was hardly any space for all three of us to undress in the bathroom. Luckily, in our secluded hangout, we had no neighbors and we undressed on the deck. Miles and I soaped our bodies clean, then Mike took a big plastic bowl, dipped it into the bucket and rinsed us off. He also helped us with washing our hair.

There was no need for any drainage. The water dripped through the gaps in the bathroom floor onto the plants below and eventually made its way into the river. Miles enjoyed the cozy shower ordeal so much that he stayed in the bath with Mike and helped him rinse the soap off his back.

It took three days for running water to come back on. Then all of a sudden the toilet began to flush properly and water dribbled out of the showerhead. Our castle was back to first-class standards.

After we had spent a relaxing day at the beach, Mike needed some action. We rented one motorcycle for the three of us. I am far too uncoordinated to learn how to ride one of those things five minutes before we are going to rent them. The either nonexistent or nonenforced traffic laws on Koh Chang and in the rest of Thailand gave us the liberty to ride around, the entire family on one bike, and we weren't given any helmets. Miles sat in the front. Each of his hands was clinging to one of the rear mirrors. He wore his blue sunglasses as sun and wind protection. I leaned around Mike, looked into the rear mirror and saw that Miles had a blast swallowing air with his mouth wide open. It made me sick watching him. I don't really enjoy motorcycle rides that much anyway. It's worse when you are squashed together on one seat and your husband takes advantage of the fact that you are entirely dependent on his mercy. He drove as fast as he could, then braked or swerved to the side over the gravel road nearly into the bushes. If he wanted to hear us scream, he sure did.

We drove past miniature spirit houses on top of posts outside the Thai houses. Many of them resemble small temples.

They were made from cement, painted and adorned with fresh hibiscus flowers and incense sticks.

The coastal road ended at a fishing village called Bang Bao. It is built on stilts and its streets are piers that stretch out onto the water. The onshore parking fee for our motorcycle was the equivalent of three and a half cents. I was glad to get off the bike, shake my legs and walk through the village on foot.

A village built above the water is quite a restrictive place for children if you think about it. No daydreaming, no stepping left and right off the bridges and walkways, or you end up swimming in murky, fishy-smelling water. If you are unlucky you have to wade through a pile of rubbish mixed with the waste from the toilets to get back on the track. Imagine growing up in such a town, playing hide and seek with your friends, chase, or trying to learn how to ride a bicycle. Just learning how to walk could turn into a neck-breaking task. At any moment you could trip up and, sure enough, the fish soup below would be welcoming you. Ironically though, I thought the place had some charm, a certain romance to it, like the smell and the rats of Venice. Miles disagreed. No wonder, since he was confined to walking hand in hand with his mother in the very center of the wooden paths watching his feet.

In one of the seafood restaurants we read about a tour to a resort on a small, secluded island, still part of the marine park. The trip sounded like it wasn't mainstream, so, we made arrangements to go to the island in a few days. Unlike the Thais, we hoped to be away from everybody for a while.

It was on a Thursday when the speedboat took us to the island of Koh Rayang Nok on which the private resort with the same name was built. When we got off the speedboat a group of Thai tourists who had been snorkeling got on the boat and took off. The resort staff greeted us and our bags were carried to a wooden cottage with a porch, two real beds in a double room and a spacious tiled bath.

I am not so sure how much of a unique Thai experience our stay on this island was, but I don't care. We were the only people staying on the island. It was fantastic. Great snorkeling, great food, great sunsets. We paddled in a kayak around the island, Miles found a swing at the beach, we played domino in the dinning room, and at night, when Miles was asleep in his tent on the porch – Mike had exiled him from our bedroom because he snored too loud – we drank rough tasting Thai whiskey with the natives who run the restaurant. We did all of this until we were forced to return to Bangkok. We had run out of cash and none of the islands had a bank or an ATM.

In Thailand, Miles had quickly accepted the otherness of his surroundings just as he had done on previous trips. But he was older now. At four, I was expecting more skepticism, questions, fear, maybe, or at least some apprehension. My expectations were wrong. Miles was positively curious. By the end of our Thai venture he knew how to get the most bizarre looking toilet to flush and how to have a nice, cool refreshing shower with just a few drops of lukewarm water dripping from a shower head and how to enjoy bucket showers. And we know now that whatever the Americans call the restroom, the Alaskans call the outhouse, the English call the loo and most continental Europeans refer to as the WC, in Thailand, this thing hasn't got a seat, and boys care less than girls.

12

The Hike

Koh Chang is an emerald green, lush, mountainous island in Eastern Thailand. In fact, it is the second largest island in Thailand and it is part of a conglomerate of 47 islands that are embedded in a National Park. In terms of its popularity with foreigners, it hasn't yet reached the ranks of a Phuket. Tourism on the islands is limited to the coastal areas of only nine islands. Their mountains and their rainforests are protected.

The guide who offered to take us on a hike through the beautiful rainforest of Koh Chang was an agile looking guy in his late twenties. He was a native, unusually tall for a Thai, but dark skinned and lean, like rest of them. He gave the impression of a healthy and well-trained person.

On a wooden table beneath a jackfruit tree he cut up some of the fruit that had fallen down. While we made conversation we ate chunks of the jackfruit which tastes like a combination of pineapple and banana. In a friendly gesture the guide stretched his hand out, inviting Miles to try the exotic fruit. James, as we were supposed to call him, seemed outgoing and pleasant enough that we wanted to spend the next day with him.

'Be at my house at seven thirty tomorrow morning,' he said. 'And bring the boy. No problem.'

He displayed the insouciance of someone who is used to taking kids in the jungle and up the mountains, or of someone who is just after the money. The latter I found unlikely.

We paid him a few dollars cash deposit and promised that we would turn up the following morning, assuming we would be able to find his place a second time. The tour guide lived along the back roads of the coastal village of Kai Bae some twenty minutes walk through high grass and past fruit trees. The neighborhood consisted of remote farms built on rich soil. The air was so incredibly hot and damp that you could feel the plants grow taller as you walked by them. Every road junction we passed looked similar to the previous one. Only the mountains behind the village told us roughly which direction to go and where to turn. But since we had found him once, I was sure we would find him again.

We had told our guide that Mike would carry Miles on his back in the toddler carrier. In trekking terms it meant that the estimated two-hour ascent would take us at least three hours. Mike and Miles both required frequent stops.

Our guide was positive. He would love to take Miles on the tour, he said. In addition, he assured us that we didn't need to worry about other tourists.

'Tomorrow I have a small group. You three and two people from England,' he explained. 'We can stop whenever you want.'

The next morning the young English couple arrived a few minutes after us. I was relieved to notice that both of them were a little overweight and, judging by what they wore, they didn't strike me as dedicated mountaineers. Rather as once-a-year hikers who would be tolerant of a father carrying his son.

Geared up to explore tropical jungle and see plants and animals we had never seen before, we waited impatiently for our guide to get ready. I was so excited to spend the whole day trekking. Incomprehensible for anyone who isn't a single parent. You don't just go hiking for a day with somebody who is not even half your size, somebody who is going to walk as fast as a duck. Therefore, I hadn't been able to go on a real hike in about two years. This morning I felt forever grateful to my husband. He agreed to carry almost 50 pounds of living mass in the obscene heat. So next time, when I trumpet about the uselessness of men after my fourth glass of red wine, remind me.

To be truthful, Mike had wanted us to go trekking by ourselves, but locals had advised him otherwise. Due to the poor terrain and the bad quality of the trails, it's worth taking a guide, they said. Glad to have had the support of the natives, I convinced Mike to go on the hike with a guide. I thought we would be safer and I hoped that the guide would be able to point out some wildlife that we wouldn't be able to spot by ourselves. Deer, wild pig, monkeys, lizards, geckos, snakes and more than 70 different species of birds roam the jungle interior of Koh Chang.

It is the tropical rainforest that draws me to a country like Thailand, since Costa Rica had converted me into a compulsive wildlife watcher. I am in love with the rainforest, its perfumey smells, the moisture and mystery of this evergreen jungle that is home to such rich ecosystems.

Once all members of the trekking group had introduced each other, the guide and his feather-light daypack assumed the lead position. He began to steer at top speed through the knee-high grass that covered the one-mile area between his house and the foot of the mountain. He ran past barking dogs that protected rundown huts, piles of garbage, and sleeping men in rough clothes. Finally, we reached the fringe of the forest and a shady jungle path took over.

Perhaps the idea of his speed-walk was to lead us out of the reach of the burning sunbeams without wasting any time whatsoever. Our troop came to a halt. I was grateful to have a moment to catch my breath. I looked behind me. There was Mike, sprinting the last few steps into the shade. His face had turned beet red.

I looked in front of me. The path was steep, and the agile young guide was already far ahead of us, tackling the steep forest wall. The English couple baffled me. They had chattered leisurely, pretending that they were annoyed by the guide's pace. Now they were quiet and only a few steps behind the guide. What was the hurry? Did they want to get rid of us?

A few minutes later we had made it about 20 feet up the hill and our group dissolved. The Thai guide was running for gold in the jungle sweat race. The English worked hard at qualifying for silver.

I had to watch where I put my feet. The ground was muddy and slippery. In the past I had been taught to carefully look at the stem of a tree before grabbing hold of it, a rule of sensible behavior in the rainforest. I climbed steadily but slowly.

Suddenly the sound of Mike's heavy breathing behind me faded. I turned around and I saw my husband exhausted, on the verge of collapse. I had never seen him like that, and he is by far the most energetic mountain climber that I know. His feet slowed down, the muscles in his well-trained legs started to shake and a continuous flow of water came shooting out of the pores of his skin. He looked kind of like a human garden sprinkler. He and Miles were soaking wet. Miles hung over the edge of the carrier giving me a guilty, 'am I too heavy'? look.

I called the guide. 'Hey. Hey. H-e-l-l-o. Could you stop, please? We need to take a break.'

I shouted again at the top of my lungs, but the bodies above us slowly disappeared, which I took to mean that either they didn't hear us, or chose to ignore us. Whatever the case, the result was the same.

My family and I stared at each other in silence, condemned to terminate the jungle expedition after thirty minutes. It was a silence of disbelief and disappointment, and, I guess, shock. It was odd to experience rude behavior in an overly friendly country like Thailand. It threw me a little.

'This man is crazy,' Mike said.

I nodded.

'I have never seen anyone run up a steep hill that fast and in this blazing heat,' Mike added.

'Hmm. Let's take Miles out of the carrier for a while,' I suggested.

'Why don't we set off through the forest with him on my back, and when we come to the open fields he can walk?' Mike responded.

At the lower part of the mountain the vegetation of the canopy forest was penetrable. I was able to point out some colorful butterflies, flowering heliconia, wild banana trees, caterpillars and lizards.

As we left the forest and continued through the grassland, hot air began to settle all around us. I knew the walk back home would be a crawl of a few hours. Maybe the abrupt end of our expedition had come as a blessing in disguise.

While Miles collected sticks and happily skipped to the right and to the left, we followed the dirt path at a moderate pace. Gradually Miles's speed reduced and his hops became small steps. We found shelter under the umbrella of a large tree. Only when I heard the unpleasant barks of dogs that had been trained to watch their property, and that tear you apart if you step over the invisible fence line, it occurred to me how peaceful the forest had been around us. Now I had to persuade Miles to walk past menacing packs of dogs that weren't kept on leashes.

Mike patted Miles on the shoulder and told him that they wouldn't do him any harm. But Miles didn't believe him and his instincts told him to be cautious. It was hard for me to make him move forward. He stood frozen stiff with tears in his eyes. His life was under imminent threat.

'How could my Mom pretend these animals are as harmless as chickens? Even my tough Dad has picked up a stick.' I am sure that was what his young brain thought.

Finally we made it around the dogs without looking at them. That alone takes some guts. We made it around the rubbish that was all around the half farms, half shelters of worn-out workers. The smell was more foul than fashionable. Then, to the right, we recognized our guide's farm. Let me assure you that we didn't stop to pay his wife the outstanding amount for our tour.

At about lunchtime we reached the village. Sometimes the challenges and limitations of adventure travel with a child seem obvious. At other times, however, it takes an unfortunate debut like that of our Thai tour guide, to make them apparent.

13

Oriental Amusement Park

Lop and his younger brother stared at Miles with penetrating curiosity. Lop, a few inches taller than Miles, had his thin long arms stretched out like a scarecrow. He wouldn't let Miles cross the footbridge that led past the Thai boy's home. 'Hi, Miles,' he saluted.

Since our accommodation was in a cul-de-sac we had to cross the footbridge over the village creek no matter where we wanted to go. Some days we crossed up to eight times back and forth. Lop was always there. Miles responded to Lop with a smile, then he jerked around and asked me if he could spend some time with the Thai kid and his brother.

At least once a day Mike and I would wait in the shade of the mango tree nearby talking, while keeping a watchful eye on Miles. I am not a paranoid mother but the footbridge over the river had gaps wide enough to resemble a horizontal ladder. Not the safest thing to play around on.

Every once in a while a lady, who I guessed to be the boys' mother, would appear from behind the massive ice box in the entrance of the shop, next to the bridge, Lop's home. Sometimes I would buy some cold water from her or a roll of toilet paper, in order to exchange smiles and nods. There wasn't much else in the shop that I wanted. However, more often than not, she wasn't to be seen.

As I continued to watch Miles and Lop I thought about the very different way that these two boys grew up. Lop was a very responsible boy who took good care of his brother. The younger one of the siblings was three and he could barely reach the rope that served as a railing. The river wasn't very wide, deep or aggressive, yet a kid who can't swim would certainly drown. Everyone knows that babies need to crawl before they can walk, but do they need to fall into a river before they learn how to swim?

Lop and his brother had two kinds of toys, the ones that nature provided for them and the ones they found in the garbage. They played with fishing nets and sticks. They spoke to the people who passed the footbridge and waited for boys like Miles to come by. On rare occasions, in the midday heat, I would see them idle in front of the TV that was mounted on the shop wall. They would rest on their backs, legs stretched out, arms crossed under their heads.

Whenever Miles came along they showed him their fish, the dead ones that they had caught earlier on or the ones alive in the river. Although Lop looked wild in his torn T-shirt he wasn't boisterous. He was very friendly to Miles and he tried to share his little world with my son, however much his limited English allowed him to do so.

During the last couple of days I had noticed that the boys had one new toy each, a bought one, a water gun. In fact, every little store had water guns for sale, and everyone was buying them regardless of age or gender. Huge, colorful water guns, easily the size of a four-year-old child. We had heard rumors about Songkhran, the Thai New Year's festival that involved people throwing buckets of water at each other, but it seemed that buckets had gone out of fashion and had been replaced by water guns. Still, we weren't convinced that we needed one as well.

The next morning at breakfast, Kevin, an English guy we had met on the beach, greeted us with several squirts of water that hit us in the back. There we sat, soaked, in a restaurant. The waiters laughed at us. Miles caught on immediately. He jumped up and wanted a gun to defend himself. So Daddy Mike took his hand and off they went to the little shop next door. They returned to the restaurant within seconds, and my son proudly presented me with his gun. It was mid-size and fluorescent green, and broke after two squirts. We nearly saw some tears, but Daddy quickly got up again and took him a second time to the store to buy a gun that looked as if it would survive a day or two of heavy action.

Still convinced that we would be able to spend this day as planned, we proceeded with renting a motorcycle. We headed south with the idea to go around the island as far as the road would take us. Twenty minutes later I was drenched from water being thrown at us, as were Miles and Mike. Worse, the ever so reliable sun disappeared behind some large clouds. I began to shiver from the wind that met us on the motorcycle and I heard Miles shivering in the front. Eventually our clothes dried and we made it as far as Baan Aow Kong Kang, a small village with no tourists. The road appeared to have come to a dead end, not on our map, but here on Koh Chang.

On our way back we stopped at a Buddhist temple and had a peek around the place. We listened to the humming sound of the chanting monks inside the *wat*. Curious faces of young boys dressed in orange robes and with shaved heads would appear at the open windows and entrance. They glanced over at us for a while and then disappeared.

Again I thought about the difference in Miles' and their lives. How extremely modest these young boys grew up. However, they didn't look bored to me, not in the slightest. They didn't look unhappy. They didn't look indifferent. They gave the impression of interested, content children who thoroughly enjoyed the company of each other. Although I couldn't imagine Miles as a monk boy, and I prefer to have him stay with me rather than at a *wat*, maybe I could instill some of the Buddhist values of modesty and compassion in him. I decided I would try.

Back on the motorcycle we re-entered the aquatic war zone with its checkpoints every few hundred meters. Attacks at these checkpoints were frequent. Gangs of teenagers and younger children made you stop by running out in the middle of the road. Once you slowed down they fired their water guns.

So that was the good-natured water throwing I had read about. We had no chance to beat off the raids, therefore, we decided to let Miles join a group of children who had their post in front of a fruit stand. Mike and I shared a pineapple and watched Miles spray bicycle riders, motorcyclists and passengers in the back of pickup trucks. Sometimes the soaked victims were armed too and fought back, then Miles would return to us dripping but still smiling.

It was time to get moving again. We came to a row of resorts, souvenir shops and restaurants. Tourists and locals had gathered along the street with water hoses and buckets filled with ice and water. It was a carnival. But the first time we got hit with a load of the iced water I cringed and Miles screamed for help. It hurt. If the original idea of the Songkhran derived from a rain-making ceremony, these guys were making damn sure that the following year there would be snow and hail storms on Koh Chang!

Cold again and in pain, I greeted Mike's suggestion to stop for lunch with enormous relief. We entered the next restaurant along the street, a pizza place, and we stayed for a few hours. There is only the one road that wraps around the island, hence there was no way we could have taken a back route to escape from the iced ammunition that was being shot at us. But, hey, everyone seemed to have a fantastic time, laughing, cheering and screaming. Miles, of course, was allowed to take part in the wild show, and again the Thai children were more than happy to share their water supplies with him. During the next hour and a half Miles didn't once turn around at us. He was busy dipping his water gun into buckets. He was involved in the world of water, in his own world, in Thailand.

The following day was a water day for Mike and myself. We went out to go diving in an old wooden fishing boat. On board were about fifteen Thai tourists with snorkel masks and fins, four young English guys with diving equipment, the instructor, the boat captain and us. We had left non-scuba fit Miles by himself on the beach, since he wasn't allowed on the boat. That probably made you nervous for a minute. Don't worry.

Thailand is children friendly and not hung up about liability and insurance issues. Miles was allowed on the boat as long as we were okay with it. And he is a good kid who can take good care of himself. He respects the deep sea and would never jump overboard just to see what would happen.

As we enjoyed the boat ride together, all of a sudden steam came from the engine along with a terrible smell, then the boat stopped. The captain, a longhaired almost Native American-looking guy, became frantic. He opened the door to the engine, jumped down into the steam, came back up, ran into his captain's hut and back and forth. Finally we heard him speak over his phone to the dive shop staff, and then we waited. We waited and waited. We swayed to the right and swayed to the left. The situation grew grotesque. There were far too many people crammed on the boat for the length of this trip. Nobody spoke, everybody was concentrating on not getting seasick. Only the instructor tried to joke with us, pretending that being stuck in the middle of the ocean wasn't a big deal. By the time the new boat came out and took us to our snorkel and dive spot I was concerned that Miles might be bored, too bored to sit on the boat for 40 minutes unattended, while we were under water. But there was no need for my concern. The captain signaled with his gestures that he would look after Miles. Two Thai women also stayed on board. They opened their handbags and pulled out handfuls of candy for Miles. I sat Miles securely in the middle of the boat and asked him to stay in that spot unless he needed to go to the toilet, in which case he would have to ask the captain to accompany him. And there he sat, in the same spot, when I came up from my underwater exploration. Back on shore, I received my Open Water certificate, Mike another stamp in his diving logbook, and Miles got a seahorse tattoo on his left arm. He well deserved it.

I guess if I was to write a brief summary about our stay in Thailand it would read like this: Islands of adventure theme park. We experienced the innovative thrills and unexpected adventures as the world's most cutting edge tuk-tuk, motorcycle, elephant and boat rides challenged all our senses. Jungle hikes and Wet 'n' Wild parties. Restaurants equipped with comfortable, on the ground, cushion chairs that have triangular backrests and make your kids feel at home. Spectacular onsite accommodation. Unlimited social inter-action for children. A hell of a country – a hell of a park.

And if you ever get to visit Koh Chang, drive out to Kai Bae Beach and have a drink in the Comfortable Bar. It opens in the late hours of the afternoon. You can watch huge crabs skit sideways across the muddy riverbanks that run alongside the bar. You can play the drums, relax on swings inside the bar, or take your drink and wander around. The walls, the ceiling and the floor are covered in fluorescent signatures and funny comments from visitors from all over the world. Somewhere amongst them it reads 'MILES'.

14

Australia
Kangaroos and Milkshakes

'We should have never come to this country!' Mike slammed his fist on the steering wheel. A bit late now, I thought, some remarkable 2,000 miles into the trip.

'The best day in Australia will be the day we leave this godforsaken country.'

Okay, he was definitely growing increasingly angry about the wrong choices that we had made. But can you be expected to make the right choices six months in advance from a distance of nine thousand and one hundred miles, unsure if in the month of May it is summer or winter in the part of the world that you are going to visit? Maps camouflage the accessibility of roads, the actual solitude of the bush, and real distances, when studied with an untrained eye.

'Well, why don't you let me drive then?' I suggested.

'No,' he mumbled.

Are all men born with a genuine mistrust in the driving skills of a woman? In the past I had driven on the left and right side of the road, whatever the traffic laws of the respective country demanded. I had driven in cities as wild as Nairobi, and never did I have an accident. Why was I supposedly not capable of driving the campervan? I guess the question was besides the point. Mike was annoyed with driving altogether although that was very much unlike him.

Being American, he loves to drive long distances. Without batting an eyelid he would consider driving from Miami to New York just for a three-day-weekend. Translated into European dimensions, that's like driving from Paris or London to Warsaw on a Friday and returning Sunday night, a crazy idea.

Mike isn't a moody person at all, but today he was in a grumpy mood and the reason was the monotony of the Australian roads combined with the slow speed of the campervan. So far he had been driving for at least six hours or more every day. The van was gobbling gas by the gallon. We had left Perth some 2,000 miles ago. To drop the van in Darwin and buy a flight ticket back to Perth sounded ideal, but the smallish, cheapish car rental agency didn't give us the option to drop the van in any other city but Perth. In very simple terms, this trip was turning out to be a boring, stressful and far too expensive nightmare. Having to sit next to your wife and watch her drive five miles slower than your own average speed would have turned this already painful adventure into a torturous inferno.

'The best thing would be to turn around and drive back to Perth. We explore Freemantle and Perth for a few days, change our plane tickets to an earlier date and fly to Fiji in, let's say, a week from now,' Mike proposed provocatively.

How logical does his proposed itinerary sound to you? We merely spend ten days on the world largest island, but since it is a damn lonely place and overpriced for misers like us we leave early and instead spend two months on the Fiji islands, which are miniscule in comparison? Now it was my turn to get aggravated. Only a further 40 miles to Roebourne. Not long and we would reach the Northern Territory. The Kakadu National Park, Darwin, the tropical wetlands, and Aboriginal culture, that's what I wanted to see and that's what I had come to Australia for. Let me tell you a secret (you might have figured it out already): Once I have made up my mind about something I stubbornly hold on to that decision regardless of the quality of the underlying rationale. And with Australia I had definitely made up my mind a long time ago, in 1974.

I was twelve years old and infatuated with my geography teacher. After telling us to learn the capital cities of all the states in the world - luckily there were only 152, or so, of them when I was a teenager - he gave us another, more stimulating task. Pick a country, find out as much as you can, prepare a portfolio and present it to the class. I picked Australia. I fear I have to admit it was because of the kangaroos. Anyway, the stuff I collected, cut out, glued, drew and wrote fell short of a doctoral thesis. Now I was eager to see this continent for real. So how could I possibly agree with Mike, although he was the more sensible parent, and also exhausted?

Even if this gruesome place had nothing else to offer but shrubs and flies, I had to see it. Perhaps we could spend more time doing things that Miles would enjoy rather than just race along the Western coast as if it was a punishment. I guess we had tried to keep Miles interested and content. It's difficult to successfully entertain a child when the geography of the country forces you to drive at least 200 miles in-between towns, through landscapes that take pride in their shortage of humans and anything remotely connected with human activity. We barely passed ten cars in a day.

Against all odds our small boy's patience was greater than ours. Due to his ability to daydream for hours he didn't always need to be doing something. On most days he was in his introvert mood, quiet. And he was intelligent enough to understand that posing the questions *Are we there yet?* or *How far is it?* would be a pointless exercise. Mike and I were glad that after seven days he was still excited about sleeping with us in the van in his little den above our heads, about spaghetti with red sauce for every dinner, and about Australia's cleverly designed playgrounds. Those of us who have traveled in the poor parts of the world will agree that the existence of playgrounds is an obvious characteristic of an industrialized, richer nation.

Nevertheless, it was Miles's wellbeing that propelled me to have another look at the road map. Not that Australia's infrastructure offers you many choices, especially when your vehicle is a shaky, low on the ground two wheel-drive.

'Let's drive one more day and see if the landscape changes and if we like it better in Broome,' I said. 'We could rest in town for two or three days and then decide what to do next.'

I suspected that the trip as we had planned it - Darwin - Alice Springs - Uluru - Nullarbor - Perth - would stand or fall in Broome. And we had to come to a decision that was fair for all of us.

Why had we repeated the errors of the first British settlers who had come to the earth's oldest continent with far too optimistic expectations? Their misperceptions of the aridity and fastness of this country had made them settle in places in which pure survival determined their daily tasks. How was it possible that we still went ahead with our original plan of driving in a slow rental vehicle along an empty and endless coastline, and later through the even more remote interior after having read Bill Bryson's 'In a Sunburned Country' on the plane? In the first few pages of his book about Australia he tells you that if you were to cut horizontally through the island you would get from bush to the outback and, about two thousand miles later, you come to bush again, and then, I might add, to a city (if you are lucky) and then to the sea. The message is clear: Australia is no Garden of Eden, despite the presence of the snake. What else did we hope for? Why didn't we change our plans in Perth, apply topographic intelligence to our map readings? I wish I could give you an answer.

Mike didn't reply to my suggestion about revising our travel itinerary in Broome. He can be deaf if he wants to. Perhaps he had already made up his mind. He stared at the road in front of him. Every so often I would check if he still had his eyes open. He always did.

'Anyway, it's Miles's turn to decide what we are going to do tomorrow,' I tried.

'Hmm. We are going to drive for most of the day tomorrow. But, yeah, once we arrive in Broome.'

Broome, Broome, Broome. I didn't know anything about the place, yet my hopes were set on it. Like Mike, I stared on the straight road in front of us. The road still looked the same as yesterday, and the day before, and the day before … but as I stopped speaking the windshield became blurry from the tears in my eyes. I didn't want to argue. Everything had begun so promising …

Several evenings ago we had sat at a small flip-out camping table surrounded by bush. The only other piece of civilization in sight was a white Toyota campervan, our home for the next six weeks. Mike got up and paced along the shrubs that circled the opening where we had made ourselves comfortable. Mike wore American length shorts, a T-shirt that he had bought in Thailand with a Buddha on the front and hiking boots. He carried a stick in one hand, just in case.

70% of Australia's land snakes are poisonous. The top ten venomous snakes in the world are found out here in the land down under. The Inland Taipan, Eastern Brown Snake, Taipan, Eastern Tiger Snake, Reevesby Island Tiger Snake, Western Australian Tiger Snake … hold on a minute. Here we were in Western Australia, about a five-hour drive north from the safe city of Perth, and besides our hiking boots there was nothing else to protect us from the bite of a snake. A feeling you have to get used to bit by bit. Every day that passes without the tragedy of a snakebite makes you feel stronger. Tonight was our first night in the bush, and I was glad that we were sleeping in a vehicle and not in a tent.

I stepped inside the campervan to get a few pencils, the composition book and the stickers that we had purchased in Perth. The evenings that we would spend deserted from distractions were ideal for open-air home schooling. We had decided that Miles would practice writing one letter of the alphabet every day.

While I watched Miles tracing and copying the letter A with childlike devotion, I began to develop a special relationship with the Australian bush that has made an everlasting impression on me. It was a love and hate relationship that was very clear-cut. During the day I would resent the dusty, crumbling red crust of the planet below our feet and wheels. Come late afternoon, the resentment would evaporate, together with the heavy and sticky air. Gaiety filled the atmosphere as the setting sun began to paint the wildest pictures on the blue canvas above our heads and on the sculptured rock formations. First with yellow strokes, than in amber and gold and then in reds and purples, until all colors drowned in the dark and were replaced by the competing beauty of millions of little star lights.

'Mom, I finished!'

His voice brought me back to what we were doing. Miles pushed his exercise book underneath my hand. I looked at his work. He had tried very hard. I rewarded Miles with a yellow kangaroo sticker that we stuck on the page. It was important that we kept up some form of schooling since at his age children start kindergarten, or at least preschool. Unfortunately we couldn't be nomads forever, and at some point soon Miles would have to enter the education system in the United States or the United Kingdom. Both bombard children earlier than ever before with what they call literacy programs. They believe it to be the solution to today's illiteracy problems. My personal view on this is that four and five-year-old children need to learn many other skills before they should be dipped into the academic world. The school systems as they are today make children part of the inevitable treadmill of academic competition far too early. By the time they are twelve years old they are fed up with formal schooling, and I would be, too. Anyway, I am losing track of my story.

A week later, we had covered almost the entire west coast of Australia. We ploughed past Roebourne, stopped at the Port Headland junction for gas, and jumped back onto the front seats of the Toyota campervan, the 'Pepsi version' of mobile homes.

'Darling, I don't think it is fair to say that the trip so far has been a waste of time and money. We have seen some cool stuff here and there.' I attempted to cheer up my husband while slurping on a bottle of water.

'To tell you the truth, I don't really care to see black emus playing soccer with trashcans when I have to drive over 1,000 miles to see them.' Mike was right. I felt the same.

'But Miles had fun watching those emus,' I retorted. 'And the Dutch people that camped next to us really entertained him with their music and their running games. It was a pleasant evening at the Exmouth Caravan Park.'

Nervously I glanced over to Mike, then I turned to Miles, who shuffled uncomfortably on the front seat.

'Miles, where is the fish chart that we bought? Let's look at it again. See if you remember the fish that you saw.'

Both our hands started digging through his rucksack. There it was. Miles ripped it out of my hand and showed me the parrotfish and the anemonefish that he had seen in the clear waters of the Ningaloo Reef near Exmouth.

'Shall I show you which fish your mommy saw?' I asked.

Both our heads hovered over the laminated diver's chart. But it was difficult. When I dive or snorkel I am much too excited. I kick my fins too fast and hardly remember much of what I see.

The Ningaloo Reef had been a hot topic of conversation inside the four walls of our van. From mid-March to mid-May whale sharks appear in large numbers at this 260 km long reef. So, on the one hand we had been fortunate to arrive at the right time at this wonderful and unique place. It was pure coincidence. The dive operators in the town of Exmouth offer to take you out to snorkel or dive with the world's largest fish. On the other hand, however, and much to our dismay, we were told that the price of the day trip is over 300 Aussie dollars for snorkeling, over 400 for diving and if they would even take Miles at all, then he certainly would have to pay, too. Full price. But Miles wouldn't snorkel in the deep ocean waters. He couldn't even swim but a few strokes. For the dive operators, this was their time to make big money. Under no circumstances was a boat space that could be occupied by a 400-dollar bum to be given away to a child. This was no Thailand, where they would have somehow squeezed skinny Miley on the boat.

'I don't regret that we didn't go diving. The Ningaloo Reef is an awesome place for snorkeling. You really don't need to dive.'

I was and I wasn't surprised that Mike had said that. Snorkeling, for a scuba diver like Mike, is like lambrucso frizzante for a wine lover. Mike would choose to live underwater if he were given the option. Nevertheless, the offshore snorkeling in the sheltered lagoons was a terrific family adventure. The reef is divine in that it is the only large coral reef in the world that is so close to the shore. Miles was able to see some small fish, black sea cucumbers and blue starfish without his mask, since he still practiced breathing with a mask and snorkel.

The amount of tourists who come to the Ningaloo Reef is small, given that it could be regarded as a more accessible version of the Great Barrier Reef. But, then again, it is in the middle of nowhere.

'I have never in my life seen so many different tropical fish swim so close to the beach.' Mike's face brightened.

'What is the name of this fish?' Miles barged in.

His finger pointed to the bottom of the chart.

'It's a trumpetfish. They are hard to see because they are so skinny. I saw them in Thailand, I think.'

If only I had known that the beach at Turquoise Bay, which enables easy access to the reef, offers no shade and no shelter from the strong winds, I would have brought tents, umbrellas, and wind-breaking nylon walls that you stick in the sand. The large Australian families, that we saw with their six kids or more in tow, pulled all this practical equipment out of their trucks and dragged it along the beach. Their skin stayed white after an entire day at the beach and they managed to barbecue in the wind without having their sausages fly off the grill.

Turquoise water, bleached white beaches of almost unnatural length, a kangaroo's head peeking over the sand dune. It sounds odd, surreal, and that's what the experience was. Where was the green vegetation? Where were the palm trees that frame any Caribbean beach and give the eye something it can linger on, so that it finds tranquility and peace?

In order to get to the Ningaloo Reef we had to cross the imaginary line called the Tropic of Capricorn. It was signposted, believe it or not, and there was a line drawn across the street. We got out of the car and posed under the sign for a ridiculous number of snapshots. Tropic of Capricorn. I had to look up the significance of it and found out that the tropics mark the sun's position in relation to the earth at two points of the year. The sun is directly overhead the Tropic of Capricorn at noon on December 21, marking the beginning of summer in the Southern Hemisphere. The area between the Tropic of Cancer in the Northern Hemisphere and the Tropic of Capricorn is called the tropics. It has no seasons because the sun is always high in the sky. I falsely associated the tropics with lush rainforests. My mistake.

'Despite Perth and the reef, I still prefer Thailand. Do you actually know how much money we have spent already in gas and camping fees for the last two nights?' Mike asked and frowned. He rarely frowns.

'I know. Much more than we can afford. That's why we eat Pot Noodles for lunch and spaghetti for dinner. Well, remember, we both thought we would be able to camp in the bush,' I said.

You really need a 4x4 to drive into the outback. In our piece of junk the wheels get stuck in the red sand.

'We should have bought a used station wagon and slept in a tent instead of renting this expensive vehicle.' Mike added another consideration to our catalogue of mistakes. 'I mean, we hoped to save on accommodation costs by renting the van and that isn't happening.'

'Yes.' I nodded.

My whimsical self wasn't going to admit that I was actually quite happy about the comfort of a small sink, an oven and arachnid-proof sleeps.

'It's such a shame that you can't really camp wild unless you are far away from the road and the towns. These rangers are everywhere and will fine you. But who am I telling this to?' I lamented.

'Unless you show them your naked butt.' Mike laughed. I laughed, too.

'Ha ha! Mama. Papa said the word butt! Ha ha!' Miles shrieked, which improved the general mood of our household.

On another evening, a few days ago, we had climbed up the stunning rock formations in the Kalbarri National Park. Below us, a river wound its way through a wide canyon. While we were admiring the beauty of the nature around us, we totally forgot about the time of the day and the bumpy dirt road that led into the park, the same road we would have to drive back on. It was almost dawn when Mike maneuvered the van around the potholes. We ended up having to find a suitable camping spot in the dark. We parked the van at a rest area the size of a gas station on the edge of a cliff five miles outside Kalbarri. Miles went to sleep. Mike and I sat outside, listened to the ocean waves, even felt a little bit of rain. We shared a bottle of red wine and played a game of chess. The darkness had lulled us into a false sense of security from the Australian law.

The next morning we woke early. Mike pulled the curtains open and started up the engine. I looked outside onto the still foggy ocean while I began to undress. We were the only ones out here. I took my nightdress off and had my naked bum temporarily pressed against the window as I was getting into my underwear. What I didn't notice was that a park ranger had pulled up in the meantime. Furious to see us camp in the wild he had jumped out of his vehicle eager to fine us. When he saw what he didn't want to see he quickly bent his head down. His face turned red, but he semi-fulfilled his mission and gave Mike a sheet of paper. Then he apologized with a stutter and decided it was all a bit much for him and his shyness that he must have inherited from his British roots. He left as fast as he could. Mike unfolded the paper and read:

This is a reminder that under section 8H of the local laws relating to reserves and foreshores, it is an offence to camp, lodge or tarry overnight within 16 kms of town boundaries. The fine for these offences is $50 per person. Thank you, Ranger.

Here we are in the emptiest part of this sparsely populated continent, in Western Australia, where two-thirds of the population lives in Perth, and you can't camp wherever your heart desires.

While we discussed the camping situation and our unfortunate choices, the temperature inside the campervan was rising to 85 degrees with the advancing of the early afternoon. I imagined crossing the Sahara desert to be similar.

'Mike, can you switch on the air-conditioning for a minute, please?'

He shook his head.

'No. Then the van burns up so much gas that we won't make it to the next gas station. We just about have enough to get to the next roadhouse.'

I wondered if car manufacturers had designed the size of the gas tank after they had measured the distances between the roadhouses on the Australian highways or vice versa. It didn't matter really.

About a hundred miles before we pulled in at the Sandfire Roadhouse, Miles showed his first signs of boredom. His personal stereo broke, so he couldn't listen to his tapes anymore. I read a few books to him, we played Go Fish, and then we talked, and then we got bored. And whenever we were totally bored, the kangaroos and the milkshakes were our only saviors.

'The first one to spot a kangaroo gets a milkshake,' Mike called out.

Miles loved the game. I guess even as an adult you don't feel you have really been in Oz until you have seen your first kangaroo. The tall, rabbit-like marsupials are everywhere, and quite easy to spot. While driving along the northwest coastal highway you will probably see more than enough, but you don't know this until you have actually spotted your first one. For some odd reason we were unlucky to the point that after two days of not seeing a single one, Miles was convinced that the lifetime of these animals had expired. They must be dinosaurs, he thought, and his parents had made up this whole spiel just to keep him entertained. Then we began to see more and more of them, and kangaroospotting became the sport that kept us from hating our trip altogether. Miles loved to win the milkshake, and Mike was in good spirits, since he took enormous pleasure in simply pretending that he saw a kangaroo. He got us worked up each time.

'Why did this German man walk around in the Australian bush?' Miles interrupted the silent game, but our eyes continued to search the horizon and edge of the road for 'roos.

'Good question,' I said.

'Because Germans are everywhere,' Mike answered with a chuckle.

'No. He didn't want to camp near anyone else so he found himself a hideout in the bush. When he heard our van drive back and forth he came to check if it was a ranger who had seen him or if it was someone else whose vehicle got stuck in the sandy ground,' I explained.

'He said that an opossum had been honking the horn in his car,' Miles proclaimed.

'Yes, that's right,' I replied, my voice expressing serious doubts.

'I would like to have an opossum for a pet.'

'How about a joey? Or one of those lizards with the huge black and purple tongues that we saw at Monkey Mia? Remember the one that licked your feet?' I asked.

'Or how about a dolphin?' Miles said in a joking manner but perhaps he was serious.

The dolphins had amazed him. They swam so close by his legs. Unfortunately, the ranger who was in charge of the Monkey Mia dolphin feeding talked for too long. Bored Miles started to throw seaweed at the legs of the other spectators who formed a line along the shallow water by the beach.

The dolphin encounter was followed by a hiking tour with one of the rangers. We all learned what a scorpion's burrow looks like. We began to distinguish the imprints of lizards and snakes in the soft red ground. Miles and another boy his age kept up with the ranger eager to look, touch and listen. They collected shells and bones. The Aussie boy took pictures with his own camera, which in turn inspired Miles. He also wanted one. Now we were in search of a simple children's camera, and I was hoping to be able to find one in Broome.

Miles yawned. Then I yawned. My husband never yawns when he drives. I put my arm around Miley and suggested, 'Why don't you sleep for a little while? I don't think we will see a kangaroo in the heat of the early afternoon. Maybe later, at dusk, that's when they become more active.'

I was wrong, there was one and another one, dead though, killed by cars. Miles turned sad. I regretted that I hadn't diverted his attention away from the road. Here in the northern part of Western Australia road kill was incredibly numerous. Sometimes we saw up to twenty or thirty dead kangaroos in a day. That's why the rental company in Perth had warned us explicitly not to drive in the dark. Under no circumstances, or you won't be covered by the insurance, they had said. The kangaroos are attracted by the beams of the lights and jump in front of the car. It happens too fast for the driver to react. Consequently, it wasn't an option for us to drive at night.

One morning we had a taste of the danger. It was early dawn. We took off from the Cape Range National Park. A joey hopped from behind a gray shrub in front of our campervan. Mike, being used to Alaskan moose that suddenly run out of the forest on to the road, reacted faster than fast and managed to avoid an emotional disaster.

Finally, Mike pulled into the Sandfire Caravan Park next to the bar, gas station and shop. We ate and then it got dark. Our flashlights in hand, we went to the washrooms. The building was damp. Something was moving. I looked at the windowsill above the sink and saw a massive toad glaring at me. Then Miles screamed with excitement. He had detected another one in the toilet. We counted five inside the washroom and another three outside. How fascinating. Oh, well. After a day on the road anything is fascinating. All I knew was that I needed a few beers and some time to think about this trip. While Miles was asleep in his overhead den and Mike was taking a shower, I sneaked to the bar and ordered a lager. I was the only person in the bar besides the young, very English-looking girl who served my drink and then disappeared. Stained newspaper clippings and bills decorated the walls. Several sleeves from men's shirts hung from the ceiling. I asked the girl about the sleeves. She told me the story. The little that I understood didn't make any sense, so I just asked for another beer. Australians are avid collectors. A town might count as few as thirty inhabitants, but rest assured they'll have a museum.

Sitting in the lonely roadhouse bar, I debated with myself what to do next. For days I had been waiting for the 'Yes, this is why everyone loves Australia' experience, the a-ha effect, that would justify all our sweat and endurance. Mike and I were both longing to experience something more exciting than a fly and ant infested miniature golf course, or ice-cold ocean water that coats you with a thick layer of seaweed while you swim in it. (Everyone who has been to Carnavon knows what I am talking about.) If we were to continue along the planned route, one thing was certain. We had to slow down considerably, so that Miles could get out of the van more often. But how could we do this without jeopardizing our departure flight out of Perth four weeks from now.

I came to the belated conclusion that the way to see Australia is either to fly from place to place, or to drive along the East Coast, or to rent a 4x4 and explore the outback whenever your call for ultimate solitude comes. If you want to do the latter with a child, you need to be extremely well prepared, and two weeks is probably more than enough.

Whichever way you chose, I guarantee you will have a better time than we had and you will be less reliant on stupid games like 'Be the first one to spot the 'roo and win a shake!'

15

NT – No more Torture

Anyone who has a basic knowledge of Australian geography knows that the letters NT stand for Northern Territory. And the city of Broome is the gateway, so to speak, to this attractive part of Australia, that is if you come from the West Coast. To be pedantic, the town is still about 300 miles away from the official border, but that's nothing in Australian terms.

After Broome it all happens. The vegetation becomes a little greener, the land looks as if it actually could be fertile, and you sense that at some point during the year a rainy season occurs. And in the far distance you see the Kimberleys, fantastic rock sculptures, mountain high.

Broome swept away much of the disillusion that all three of us had experienced so far. In fact, we began to get more involved in Australia. We interacted with the people around us and our status as the 'alien-visitors-in-the-van' transformed into the 'engaged-travelers-leaving-the-van-and-speaking-to-people.'

It was a Saturday evening. Mike and I had been to the Broome Open Air Cinema, the oldest in Australia. What a mind-blowing setup! A saloon type entrance led to a smallish theatre filled with rows of deck chairs. You got yourself a drink, selected your seat and kicked back to enjoy a movie against the backdrop of moon and stars. Since I don't even remember which movie we saw I figure that I must have enjoyed the romantic ambience of the place more than whatever they showed on the huge screen.

Miles slept in the front row. No, sorry, in front of the movie theatre in our camper. Before you start freaking out and try to report me to the police, take a deep breath and let me reassure you that it's too late. Miles was knocked out from a day full of activities and movement. He wouldn't have appreciated being woken up by the police. Of course, we had locked the doors of the vehicle and parked it right in front of the well-lit movie theatre entrance. Twice during the show Mike sneaked out to check if he was still asleep.

Back at the Roebuck Bay Caravan Park, Mike and I sat outside in our camping chairs and continued to admire the Australian sky. Everyone around us was still up and doing something. Some played cards or read. Others did their laundry. Our neighbors ate their supper. We looked at each other and agreed that our family had had a splendid day.

The Broome Saturday hadn't been an ordinary Saturday. On ordinary Saturdays you need to be doing all the things you don't get to do during the week and you don't want to do on a

Sunday, so you crawl out of bed earlier than you wish to and it doesn't feel right. You shop for groceries, clean the house and the garden, maybe the garage, too. The car might need an oil change. The child needs a haircut, father a new pair of shoes. Mom needs to dye her hair.

How do I communicate with my child on an ordinary Saturday?

I may say, 'Get ready we want to leave ... No, you can't take two handfuls of toys to the shop. You will loose them ... Get in the car, please. Come on, we have a lot to do ... I know you are thirsty, but let's open the juice boxes at home. I am driving. Go thirsty for a few minutes. Okay? I don't want a mess in the car ... Don't step with your dirty shoes on the kitchen floor. I have just cleaned it ... Why don't you play by yourself for a while?'

I hope that doesn't sound familiar.

On that Saturday in Broome we also had to shop for food, fill the van with gas and clean the windshield, do the washing up, and that was about it. But we were on vacation, and that made all the difference. The way I spoke to Miles was less urging, and doing household chores didn't make us as irritable.

Miles decided to go to Roebuck Bay Beach while Dad cooked breakfast, but Dad postponed the breakfast preparation because he wanted to join us. Early in the morning Roebuck Bay Beach is covered with hundreds of hermit crabs. Miles didn't notice them at first, but when he came out of the water and saw his feet surrounded by myriads of crabs he jumped. Then he lifted his elbows up to shoulder height and step-danced. His mouth made all sorts of vowel sounds until I rushed for assistance. I moved him away from the masses of moving shells to a quieter spot where some children were busy building a sandcastle. They had caught dozens of crabs with their buckets and sentenced them to life imprisonment in their sandcastle. Miles observed the children quietly before he joined in. His little hands helped reconstruct the walls that some of the bigger crabs had destroyed in their effort to escape. And later, after about half an hour into the game, his fingers lifted the runaway crabs by their portable homes to put them back into their prison cells.

After breakfast we went shopping in an air-conditioned supermarket. As much as I despise air-conditioning for its detrimental effects on our environment and health, that particular morning I spent an excessive amount of time in the store strolling up and down the cool aisles. I bent over the freezer section and sucked in the even cooler air. No flies, cool air. It felt like heaven. Australia's heat bothers your mind because there is no shade; there is nowhere to hide from it. I observed Mike and Miles. These impatient male shoppers didn't seem to mind idling through a supermarket. Did we enjoy the same things? Surrounded by the largest selection of food since Perth, we decided to cross Spaghetti dinners off the menu, at least for a while, and we bought barbecue meat for lunch. Then we found a camera store. We bought Miles the much-desired kids camera and some film.

At lunchtime we joined our neighbor's *barbie* with our bring-along-meats. The neighbor's family consisted of three generations of Australians traveling together.

'G'day,' a mom with a baby on her lap welcomed us.

Miles had already escaped with his new playmates. As soon as Mike and I sat down we were engaged in the travelers' foreplay, as I call it. We gave information about where we come from, where we work, what we were doing in Broome, and how old Miles was. When they had run out of questions to ask and there was a moment of silence I captured the opportunity. I wanted to find out what authentic white Australians who came from the East Coast thought about their holiday experience on the West Coast.

Boring, dull, lots of driving, nothing happening. Were they going to say that? Will they warn us? Don't travel through the center, it will only get worse. And under no circumstances cross the Nullarbor. There are no trees for hundreds of miles. No trees. That's what the word means, goddamnit!

My assumptions proved wrong. The terms with which they described their country were the same I would use to describe Eastern Africa. The rich wildlife, the abundance of birds, the serenity of the landscapes ... Australia, Australia, country of stunning beauty!

Let's face it. There are some weird animals and plants in Australia because they have developed for far too long in isolation from the rest of the normal world. But birds? Didn't they mean flies? I hadn't seen any birds, besides a flock of pinkish Cockatoos. I am no birder, but in Kenya or Costa Rica, for example, birds are right in your face. In Western Australia I wouldn't know where to look. Where would you look for birds in the semi-desert? I saw magpies on leafless trees.

The Aussies' devoted love for their ancient continent, for rocks and stones that are millions of years old, became apparent, and it isn't even that surprising once you think about it. Where did the white Australians migrate form? Who were they? They were British convicts and could have ended up far worse than in the land down under. These people were grateful, modest, happy with a cup of tea. Sarcasm aside, the conversation left an imprint on my thinking about Australia, and I have a feeling on my husband's, too. Sometimes people have to remind you that your glass is half full and not half empty.

Broome, an old pearling port, features the best beach in Western Australia, Cable Beach. As the red fireball — so says Miles - crawled down from the sky and dipped into the Indian Ocean, we held running competitions on the 22 km long and very wide beach, then we sat on a rock catching our breaths, and we watched the silhouettes of tourists who rode on camels against the spectacular sunset.

Three memorable days later we were on the road again, swerving around road kill. Once per day one of these massive train trucks passed us. No matter how close we steered to the ditch, the entire van would shake as the trucks thundered by.

Now, and probably never again in our lives, we were heading toward Darwin. I blamed our Australian camping neighbors for it. I was curious to see if I could detect the beauty of the inhospitable land the same way they did. And since Miles had thoroughly enjoyed hanging out with the Aussie kids, we figured we would just pay up and stay on campgrounds so he could see more of them and less of his parents.

After a full day in the Territory Wildlife Park, Miles decided Australia was his favorite country. During a wildlife show a barking owl flew right over his head. We watched monitor lizards swim, pelicans being fed fish, we lamented the orphaned joey whose mom had been killed by a car, we walked through a tunnel aquarium, and we observed dingos, Dad's favorite animals. Late afternoon we drove to a tastefully landscaped caravan park just outside of Darwin. As soon as we passed the pool Miles wanted to go for a swim. He put on his swim shorts at 50 miles per hour and ran down the path. Everywhere we go he remembers instantaneously how to get to the pool, the restaurant, if there is one, the toilets, and the washrooms. Utterly amazing. I tend to take Miles with me so I don't get lost. This time Mike went with Miles to the pool while I did our laundry and cleaned up the mess in the van.

I heard screaming and splashing in the far distance. Curious, I joined the boys. Miles was in the pool with three Australian families trying to catch a ball while struggling to stay afloat. He did a few strokes more than he was used to and probably didn't even notice it. He was so involved in the game. Then his hands reached for the edge of the pool, he was gasping for air. I said something to Miles about the water being deep, but he didn't hear me. Mike and I sat by the pool and watched him. Miles didn't see us either. And I didn't blame him. We had been with him for 24 hours. Sometimes you just have enough of each other's company.

Miles snatched the ball from the Aussie kids and threw it to one of the fathers. The man liked Miles and threw it back to him. In the end, the group of swimming adults played ball with Miles while their own kids looked bored. Miles used to display an almost clownish friendliness, and he looked cute enough to get people's attention within a few minutes. Most of the time we profited from the ease with which he met people and this time was no exception. One of the family fathers invited us to join their *barbie* later that evening.

The group around the grill and the coolers with chilled beer was 100% 'Darwinian'. An accountant with his wife and four children, a banker with his wife and four children, and a journalist with his girlfriend. I could swear that there were far more than just eight children running around in the semi-dark.

In conversation I learned that they had taken several nephews and nieces along camping. Huge families, the outdoors, meat and beer, that's quintessential Australia. Miles played soccer with the flock of children, and in-between the shots and passes he grabbed pieces of meat off the grill. When it got dark he was given a flashlight and he bounced in and out of the caravans, tents and small wooden cabins that the families had rented.

We talked about the cyclone that had destroyed over 50% of Darwin's houses in 1974. They told us how much they loved living in today's cyclone-proof Darwin. The more they talked about the city, the larger it got in my mind, only to realize the next day, when we walked through Darwin, that the city center is only one street, Mitchell Street, about ten blocks of it.

'Darwinians' hop over to Bali like Floridians hop over to Jamaica or Californians leap to Hawaii. It's affordable and close enough to go for just a few days, we learned. Then we were interrogated about Miles. How many languages did Miles speak? (He said three: English, German and Spanish. What a show off!) And why had we come to Australia?

Good question, we had come to buy land. But now, we weren't quite so sure if we could hack it, life in the land down under, I mean. Too many mosquitoes, too many flies. You never get a break. It was very late when we left the party and walked through the high grass to the van. Miles was so exhausted he sleepwalked half of the way.

Another campground that invigorated our spirits is situated just outside the Litchfield National Park. It is one of those caravan parks that is blessed with the presence of a swimming hole filled with cool, fresh water. There are a few in the Northern Territory. After a hot day in the car or bush, you name it, it's hot everywhere, you wade into the swimming hole and, believe me, you don't care if there is a 'salty' swimming in it just waiting to rip your legs and arms off and devour you like a snack.

Given that the dangerous saltwater crocodiles can survive in freshwater and sometimes travel over long distances, even overland, to get to water, swimming in these water holes may be classified as daring, borderline with dangerous. However, these swimming holes are traditionally visited by the less dangerous freshwater crocodiles. Underwater gates make it difficult for the crocs to enter these natural pools from the river. Rangers check the water on a regular basis to make sure that swimmers are safe.

After supper Mike, Miles and I went for a walk around the swimming hole when, all of a sudden, Mike pointed to a bat colony of at least a hundred bats hanging above our heads and in the trees around us as far as our eyes could see. Unable to detect the beauty in a bat, I stood and observed them for quite some time. They were the Draculas of the rodents, hanging upside down, too ugly to be birds, but striving to have a better life than ordinary mice. Miles was fascinated. He saw 'Stellaluna' in real life. One after the other they began to stretch their leathery wings, preparing their bodies for their nightly hunt. They yawned and stretched and looked around, then huddled up again in their wings just to sleep for another ten minutes or so before getting up. So much like me in the mornings. I began to like them.

Most four or five year olds that I have met in the States remember their birthdays by the different names of fast-food joints. Third birthday at Burger King, fourth at Mac Donald's and so forth. Miles remembers them by countries. Fourth in England, fifth in Australia, ...

On the morning of his birthday, we happened to be at the Edith Fall's campground. We enjoyed it so much that we stayed at it twice, on our way up the Stuart Highway to Darwin and on our way down toward Alice Springs. Mike and I had hidden Miles's birthday presents in and around the campervan. He went on a treasure hunt, finding an activity book about Australian animals, a T-shirt with a crocodile on it, a plastic frilled lizard that squeaks and a bag with water balloons. A laughing kookaburra watched Miles searching for his presents.

After breakfast we jumped in the car and took off to visit a crocodile farm. Miles was excited to take photographs with his own camera and he did a fantastic job, given that it was only the second time that he had used it. The first time he took photos at the Keep River National Park, mainly of other tourists, and we had to teach him that he couldn't take pictures of people without asking first. At the crocodile farm one obvious motive for his photos were the huge salties that were basking in the sun. These huge reptiles can get as big as 23 feet long. While Mike and Miles ate 'Crocburgers' for lunch I took a walk through the gift shop and detected a folder with newspaper clippings about crocodile attacks. The stories were extremely worrying. I remember one about a man riding his bicycle along a road and a croc jumping out from a nearby river and going after the man's legs. He tore the helpless man off his bike and killed him.

Thirty years ago, when salties were near extinction, hunted for their precious skulls and skins, Australians began to protect the reptile in an overly caring manner. Salties are protected not only in national parks but also in neighborhoods, with the

THE GLOBE TODDLER 197

effect that they are striking back, frequently and viciously. Outback cattle stations are the victims of the attacks, and, here and there, a tourist.

'It's the head and the eyes that I find most fearsome, especially when they are chewing on a dead cow,' said a farmer to a reporter from a Scottish newspaper.

Splendid. Encouraging stories for anyone who travels the Northern Territory. Aren't you just happy to be here instead of in Southern Australia, where divers get eaten alive by sharks? And although we had watched a salty swallowing several whole chickens with feathers, we were still free of any symptoms of crocophobia by the time we left the 'Top End'.

16
Eddie

White Australians are the kind of people you meet in large groups when you backpack around the world or work in summer camps in the United Kingdom. I had done both and met plenty of them. I still remember most of their names. There was Phil from Perth, Andy, and a guy they called Maggot from Brisbane. There was Carl from Sydney, then the girls, Lynn and Vanessa from Canberra. They were outdoorsy, straightforward and extremely likable people. Now, as we were approaching Alice Springs it struck me that I had never met anyone who came from this urban area. In practical terms, this meant I had no number to dial and knew no one to show us around town. And nobody in Alice Springs could be put in the situation to regret that he gave his phone number to some crazy German girl fifteen years ago.

The Alice, as they call it, is the largest city in the Red Center. I was curious to see what it would be like and what kind of people would choose to live in such an isolated place. No more than several hundred people lived in this settlement along the Stuart Highway until the 1950s. Lately, however, it has experienced a population explosion and, consequently, it counted over 25,000 inhabitants when we arrived.

We drove and walked around the Alice. I didn't think it was that special. I certainly couldn't imagine living here myself. It kind of lacks the charm of a city like Perth. Maybe because it has no water. I mean, in addition to the fact that it hardly ever rains, there is no lake, river or ocean that could make this place more agreeable to the mind. Despite the mediocrity of the city we had some interesting and entertaining experiences in and around Alice Springs that are still fresh in Miles's memory.

230 miles north of Alice Springs lies the Devil's Marbles Conservation Reserve. It was the name of the place that made us focus on it. Conveniently located right next to the highway, we thought we would stay the night before driving into the Alice the next morning. As soon as Mike turned the van off the street and toward the parking area, which is also the campground, I thought we had just entered a Magritte painting. Gigantic round and oval boulders that fill the picture surrounded us. Wherever you looked you saw oversize rocks scattered, forming small heaps, or some balancing delicately on top of others. I could feel their enormous weight simply by looking at them, but my mind was unable to conceptualize why they weren't tumbling. Without a doubt the supernatural arrangement of the smooth, round boulders must have been the work of Lucifer rather than of an Isaac Newton. The

Aboriginal people say the marbles are the eggs from the Rainbow Serpent.

You are permitted to enter the site and make it your playpen. It's not like Stonehenge in Southern England where thousands of meters of rope make sure that you aren't in touching distance of the rocks. Mike, Miles and I climbed the boulders, hid behind them, pretended we were Obelix and carried them on our backs. We posed under the weight of one, on top of another one, heads up, heads down, peeking around the sides, while Mike's camera clicked rhythmically.

Then it was Mike's turn to play around in the Garden of Marbles. He flew up to incredible heights, pretending to fall down, and that way he amused Miles, but probed the constitution of my nervous system. I opted to hold Miles's hand to prevent him from following his Dad. In touch with nature, we sat up high, our backs leaning against the cool rock behind us. Then we laid on our bellies, real quiet, and we watched wild cats scurry by and kangaroos graze.

We cooked sausages for dinner and stretched out on our sleeping mats that we had rolled out on square wooden raft-like constructions. Built on four legs, 2 feet in the air, they keep you off the ground, safe from ants and other biting creatures. You find them on almost any campground in Australia. Mike was explaining the stars and planets to us, when a group of young guys who looked like the devil's sons came to invite us to their fireshow, as they called it.

Well, who would have thought, live entertainment in the middle of nowhere! A bunch of elderly Australians had already gathered in a circle, their deck chairs neatly set up exactly 2 feet and 2 inches from one another. The performance started promptly with a bang. Hellish music blasted out of a battery-powered stereo. Two of the guys took turns swinging balls of fire on heavy iron chains through the air. Punk, funk, what a circus. The fire, the stars, the smell of gasoline and a bunch of old people watching, shaking their heads in disapproval whenever the 'F' word came firing out of the stereo. But the old folks didn't leave. Where would they go anyway? It was impossible not to hear the music, even if they had shut the windows of their mobile homes. So they stayed until the bitter end and applauded politely.

Thankfully, Miles's ears are still oblivious to swear words. Moreover, the volume of the music was so deafening that there was no need to worry. At the end of the show the performers put a hat on the ground. Miles refused to give them the dollar bills we had shoved in his hand, although he said that he liked their tricks and I could tell he was impressed. Children make their own choices and sometimes we don't comprehend their reasons.

The Wintersun Caravan Park on the outskirts of Alice Springs was a less eventful place. We were allocated a shady slot on a grassy camping area. After a quick visit to one of the local supermarkets we got organized, cleaned the van, set up chairs and a table, got Miles's toy box out, a carton from a grocery store, decided that there was not one toy in it that we hadn't played with a million times already, took showers and did the laundry.

The plan was to relax, nothing else, but to relax. Later on, we headed into town, went for a stroll around the touristy pedestrian area. Several shops sell Aboriginal arts and crafts, and we were toying with the idea of buying a didgeridoo. But since these musical instruments aren't easy to travel with due to their weight and length, and since we were afraid that the mouthpiece, which is made from native honeybee wax, would get ruined if we were to ship it, we bought a CD instead. It plays a rare but appealing combination of flamenco mixed with the deep and hollow sounds of the didgeridoo.

The Alice was the first place where we saw large numbers of Aboriginals with frizzy 6 to7-inch long hair that sticks out in all directions as if electrocuted. Several women had facial hair like men. Poorly dressed, they wandered the streets during the daytime, which probably meant that they were jobless, since they didn't seem to be going anywhere. They painted a sad picture that didn't compliment the city.

At a gas station we witnessed the cashier throwing a group of Aboriginal children out of his shop. The kids in ragged clothes had been begging in the streets for some change. With the coins squeezed tight in their little hands they wanted to buy some sweets, but the cashier was annoyed by their presence.

'Thieves. All of them, thieves,' the old man said and shook his head.

This wasn't the only time during our trip that we saw Aboriginal kids being ordered to leave a shop.

For dinner we ate out in one of the many restaurants in the Alice. We tried authentic Australian *tucker*, kangaroo and wallaby. At first, Miles seemed indecisive about trying kangaroo, but being a meat-lover at heart, he overcame emotional barriers of that sort quickly and dug in.

The next day we woke early to visit the School of the Air. Miles banged with his feet against the walls of the van well before the alarm went off. He was thrilled about going to school in Australia and meeting lots of children. Although I had explained to him as best as I could that the School of the Air is a different kind of school and that he wouldn't meet the students because they lived far away in the bush on their cattle farms, Miles didn't believe me. A school without children didn't seem to make sense to him.

What looks like a small elementary school from the outside is, in fact, the world's biggest classroom. As we entered we were welcomed by the decorative arts and crafts of elementary school children and their outstanding academic achievements that are stuck to the walls. We stopped in front of a huge glass window that allowed us to observe what was going on in the broadcasting studio. The teacher sat in front of a microphone. She greeted the children in the outback via HF radio transceiver. A chorus of children from kindergarten to Year 7 - that is all levels of an elementary school - greeted her back. She began the morning assembly. We heard a girl singing. Then the voice of another one. Some chanting. The teacher continued with the first lesson of the day. She responded to each student in the class individually. She knew their voices. She even detected who is absent when the class answers in chorus. She put names to the shy, the shrieking and the boisterous, the male and the female voices that sneaked back to her over the radio transceivers. I have no idea how she did with all the crackling noises going on.

The School of the Air covers an area of 500,000 square miles. It reaches out to the lonely stations in the bush and gives these children a personal access to education that goes far beyond education by correspondence. In 1951, when the first School of the Air opened in Alice Springs, teachers used the radio facilities of the Royal Flying Doctor Service in order to transmit their lessons. Today, some of the infrastructure is replaced by live lessons via satellite. Once a year the teacher drives his 4x4 along silent dirt roads into the outback to visit the children whose only social interaction is with their family members. The nearest neighbors might be 30 or 40 miles away. The young children that attend the School of the Air come together for a sleepover and fun activities two times a year. A lifestyle that would make many of us go nuts, especially those parents among us who claim that daycare friendships among two-year-old screamers exist. The idea that a toddler grows up in the presence of his parents only, would be inconceivable for them.

In the afternoon we drove to a local car dealer to finally have our side mirror fixed. On our way from Darwin to Alice Springs we stopped midway for an oil change. The car mechanic who dealt with it drove our campervan onto a rack, but not quite straight. So when the rack lifted the van fell to the side and one of the side mirrors ripped off. A new one was ordered and we were told to pick it up at a garage in Alice Springs. The apologetic car mechanic was utterly embarrassed and hid his face behind the toy camel that he ended up giving Miles. The camel, in its karate outfit, became our travel mascot, and although you associate camels with the Middle East rather than Australia, these great animals of transport have actually played an important role in the history of Australia, in particular in the region were we where.

In the 19th century, Afghan traders brought the first camels to Australia. The camels acted as trucks and trains and helped to build the inland of this continent. They carried the supplies for mines and sheep stations. They connected remote settlements with one another. When the real trucks and trains took over, the camels were released into the wild. Today, an estimated 200,000 camels live in the outback. Some of them are wild and some live on farms. The camel farms use their camels for camel safaris or they try to make some big bucks training them for the camel races. The most famous annual camel race takes place in Boulia, a tiny settlement less than 100 miles northeast of the Simpson Desert. The prize money for the race stands at 30,000 Australian dollars.

With camel racing being a fast growing sport in the outback there is a surprisingly large number of Australians who are camel mad. They are as mad as to arrest someone who rides on his camel drunk. It was reported in 1998 that Richard Church used to ride his camel at a speed of four miles per hour, often after he had had a few beers. One day, he was arrested. I wonder how many lives he actually threatened in the outback by riding drunk.

It was about time that my family spent a day on a camel's back. South of Alice Springs, in a community called Stuarts Well, a camelman by the name of Noel Fullarton established a camel farm in the late 1970s. Today, his family runs the farm. It is a place where children can go on camel rides around the track, stand around in the barn and observe the camels and lamas, and there is a small farm shop that sells refreshments.

The day after all of Mike's shorts were stolen from the washing line at the Wintersun Caravan Park we left to camp in the bush near Stuarts Well. Haunted first by flies and then by mosquitoes, we spent most of the evening in the closed surroundings of our rental Toyota as if we never got to spend any time in it. At the crack of dawn we rumbled across the highway to Noel's camel farm to meet with a guy called Dan who was going to take us on a one-day camel safari into the Rainbow Valley.

Long hair tied into a ponytail, a long beard, a hat with a wide brim, a checkered shirt and denim jeans: that was Dan. Too skinny to be a Vietnam veteran, and too energetic for a hippie. Somewhere in-between though, that's the look of your typical outback dweller. Talkative, because there aren't many people to talk to besides the tourists, overwhelmingly friendly, and in tune with nature.

Dan was happy to take Miles on the trip and he gave him his own camel to ride. Miles was euphoric, which expressed itself in the great leaps and jumps that he performed in circles around the four camels that patiently sat on their knees in the sand and chewed. They were completely oblivious to Miles's breakdance. I guess camels aren't very emotional animals. Dan had already saddled the dromedaries. All that was left to do was to tie Miles's camel, Eddie, to Dan's camel, just in case.

Our four human, four camel caravan rode up and down the hills of the Rainbow Valley. Towers of ochre, red iron and gold sandstone layers paraded on both sides of the track. It was hot, and as soon as your camel stopped to rip some leaves off a tree branch or to break off an entire branch, flies pestered you. They flew into your nostrils, ears and eyes. That's the prize you have to pay for intoxicating your mind with the natural beauty and the absolute tranquility of the valley.

Since camels are famous for doing whatever they please, we were lucky in that our four hairy friends liked Dan and showed obedience. After the first five minutes Miles had completely recovered from the shock of sitting high up on the back of a gurgling and burping animal. He regained his voice and rattled on and on. He showed Dan every bird that he saw and talked his ear off about the trees and potential snakes, Eddie this and Eddie that, and about how much he loved camels.

We stopped to rest in the shade of a huge rock. Dan tied the camels to a tree and he and Miles picked leaves for them. Then Dan made a small campfire and boiled some water in his pot, or *billy*, as they say here. He served us sweet tea and we had sponge cake. Miles got juice. Intrigued by his camel, he jugged down the juice and spent the rest of the time checking on Eddie. Never too close to Eddie's monstrous teeth and fleshy lips, Miles held out leafy branches and dry grass.

On our way back to the farm Dan saw a group of camels in the far distance. He told us that he had released those camels in the wild some weeks ago. We rode over to see them. They stood in the shade of a tree. As we came closer they gave us dopey looks, with their dark brown eyes framed by diva-like eyelashes. Then Eddie got too carried away with eating tree branches. Dan told Miles to make it move by shouting 'Walk up' and kicking it in the side. Dan was patient with Miles, the way you have to be when you train camels, and he gave him the confidence to handle Eddie. Of course, being tied to Dan's camel, Eddie wasn't given much choice but to eventually move along. The beasts that never get tired of masticating their cud, chewed and chewed while they took us past a flock of black cockatoos with red tails, herds of black cattle and out of the Rainbow Valley back to the highway.

The trot of the camels was soothing. The humpy animals are called ships of the desert with good reason. We rode the waves and sailed the seas of red sand on their backs for six hours, enough time to get a little taste of the outback and to indulge. Enough for Miles to believe that Eddie would remember him forever.

17

Uluru – Why Walk?

Bush Flower
Seeds burst open under sun and rain.
Honey flows from colorful flowers.
Song cycles tell the story of new
Life for the land.
-Australian, source unknown

Try taking a five-year-old for a stroll through the stores of a
giant shopping mall. Try taking him sightseeing in a metropolis
like London or Washington, D.C. Walk through a museum of
modern art with him. Or just through a grocery store. I am
positive you won't call it your lucky day. Initially, while the kid
is still feeling energetic, you will find yourself chasing him or
her. Mine enjoys hiding in clothes stores between women's
dresses or men's coats so that I stand yelling his name, watched

by the general public shaking their heads at me. Later on, however, the kid's hand pulls yours in the opposite direction, forces you to reverse or walk at a snail's pace, and all the while he complains that he is hungry, thirsty, tired, bored and fed up. Then he blackmails you. He threatens you. You either buy one of the balloons, a soft drink, a chocolate bar and a new toy, or life will be hell. He will show you up, throw himself on the floor and scream at the top of his lungs.

Miles whines and moves extra slow when I want to hurry. It must be the asphalt, the concrete, or smooth tile under his feet that does that to him. Unless a toy store window or a shelf filled with sweets crosses his path. Then he comes to a complete standstill for hours. If I weren't lifting him along by putting my hands under his armpits, I would be standing in one spot for eternity. Against my principles I buy him something, something small made from plastic that is a total waste and will break the next day, or something that will rot his teeth.

But whenever my son's shoes tread on rocks, stones, dirt or sand he almost runs. Nature has an uplifting, energizing effect on him that makes him accelerate. During our stay in Australia we took advantage of his affinity for nature and we went on moderate hikes every evening. And at the end of these short walks through Wonderland there would always await some reward-surprise, like the sighting of wallabies, a refreshing waterhole to swim in, a waterfall, or the grunting of wild boars that would chase us back to our campervan.

When you walk around Uluru, the biggest monolith on earth, you are in the heart of Australia, in the desert, and there are no toy stores or sweet stands to distract your kid. You could toss a handful of survival sweets in your daypack just to keep him or her going, but that's entirely up to you.

The walk around the sacred rock of the Anangu, the Aboriginal people, represented quite a number of challenges for Miles, despite the fact that he was a well-trained hiker for a five-year-old. The circuit walk is almost six miles long. Some, like us, make it in six hours, but most complete the walk in three to four. Shelter-providing trees are a rarity. Even the 1,115-feet monolith doesn't throw as much shade on the earth as you would expect. So you are walking in the burning sun and you wish you had brought an umbrella.

In fact, already after the first few minutes Miles began to complain. I was startled and at the same time annoyed. We still had the entire walk ahead of us, why did he start off unmotivated? What was wrong with Miles? Did he suffer from stomachache or did his feet hurt in his shoes?

'Why are we still walking?' he kept mumbling to himself. 'Why are we still walking?'

'What are you saying?' I quizzed him. 'We'll be walking all day long. I did tell you that, didn't I?'

It took me a while to understand that Miles thought walking around a rock, since that was the word we used when we referred to Uluru, couldn't take very long. After the initial misunderstanding was cleared Miles walked to our first stop, the Kantju waterhole, agile like a gazelle, happy to be alive and moving. We sat down and I thought this really is a site of peace and tranquility.

The Mala people, the ancestors of the Aboriginal people, used the Kantju waterhole as a quiet place. It was one of the few shady spots on our walk. We gave the little man's legs enough time to regain their strength before we continued the hike.

For the next part I planned to involve Miles in a conversation. This would keep his mind busy, although he was still engaged with his environment. His eyes were searching the terrain for cool looking pebbles and for lizards. He was such a balanced kid in nature. More content, I would say, not tense or edgy, than when confined.

The hike was very tranquil. We hardly met any tourists. For most of the time it was just us small people at the foot of this immense rock that rises abruptly out of the terra firma. Miles trod on behind Mike and I trod on behind Miles. To the left of us Uluru, then all of a sudden we changed sides with the rock as we came around its corner and now it was to the right of us. We gave up the hope for shade. Nothing else but gray bush that grows out of the earth's crust surrounded us. The small path that we followed wound like a snake through the shrubs, and it reminded me that we had to watch where we stepped.

Every once in a while I told Miles to look up and study the ever-changing face of the single red standstone monolith. Wind and rain over millions of years gave Uluru its personality. Caves, crevices and holes in the otherwise smooth slopes that tell you the stories of its people, the Aboriginal people, aren't visible on the picture postcard photo of Ayers Rock.

Miles was still going strong. It was me who was incredibly thirsty. Just the look of this arid land dehydrated me. The dust and the flies made me feel dry and deserted. It was me who had wanted to do this walk in order to get at least a slight feeling of the amazing and much too under-rated culture that has had this rock as its centerpiece of tradition, religion, ceremonies and history for many thousands of years. We trudged on. I told Miles about the Aboriginal people and their children.

'They didn't have shoes like you. They walked barefoot, and their feet were cut up by the razor blade-sharp spinifex.'

Miles nodded, a sign that he was listening.

'You know, not all to long ago a man called Jeremy Long went into the desert some 570 miles from Alice Springs. The land over there looks just like the land here around the rock. Well, he visited the Pintubi people, a type of Aboriginal, in the Gibson Desert. The children of these people grow up in small families. They maybe have one or two brothers and sisters. They are nomads. It really means that they don't have a house like we do. They have their weapons with which they hunt and that's about it. No toys, no clothes, …'

'No bed,' Miles barged in.

'Exactly. They sleep on the ground. And, as you know, in the nighttime it can get very cold. So, what they do is, they make a fire and sleep very close to it. Sometimes so close that they burn their skin,' I explained.

Far removed from the world of the Aboriginal desert nomad, back home we sleep on soft mattresses, head cushioned, on clean white sheets. As modern parents we are advised to rethink taking our newborn baby into this comfortable bed with us. The baby might die of suffocation. It might get trapped in-between the bed and the wall. The things we worry about seem pathetic when we look at the overall picture, when we look at how children without the same privileges grow up. How far removed are we from nature? Parents don't suffocate their babies. I slept with Miles in my arms in a single bed many, many nights. Had I ever squashed him, he would have screamed. The human contact, the closeness to his mother, nourished his soul. He felt safe. He was safe. Safer than the little boys and girls who have to sleep without a blanket under the cold, dark sky in the Gibson Desert. Yet, I don't think that these children of the Stone Age are frightened. They certainly aren't as removed from their parents as many of our babies who are put into their own crib in their own bedroom just a few days after their birth.

'What do the kids eat?' Miles asked.

'Well, I guess they eat rabbits with fur, lizards, goannas, mice and berries. Not something you would like to try, right?'

'Eeehhhhh, that's disgusting!'

'Oh, goannas are delicious. They taste just like chicken,' I joked, but I wasn't lying. I had eaten barbecued iguanas, which are similar. 'You like most of the things that you grow up with. Maybe those kids think that ice-cream and French fries are disgusting.'

'No way,' Miles disagreed vehemently.

'I remember the first few times you ate ice cream, you didn't like it. You told me it was too cold and you spat it out,' I said, and then I continued to describe the desert children's life.

'Children your age know how to cook their own food and know how to make their own campfire. Their moms don't cook for them. They are very independent at an early age. They learn how to walk long distances when they are very young. Then they are taught how to hunt so that they can go out and catch their own food. They learn survival skills, not the ABC's or numbers. I don't know what they play with. I guess they have little time to play anyway. And they certainly don't go to school. There is no school in the desert and the children are busy walking with their parents to find waterholes and hunting for their dinners. You just go into the kitchen and open the fridge door for food and drink. They can't. If they don't catch anything, or if their parents don't find water, they go hungry and thirsty.'

'Why don't they have a fridge?' Miles asked.

'Because they don't have houses. The little kids are very brave. Besides being hungry and thirsty sometimes, they also suffer from illnesses and injuries that can't always be treated by their parents. And they don't really have doctors to go to. So on certain days they walk in pain. But it makes them very, very tough.'

'I think I am stronger,' Miles says, and flexes his arm muscles Popeye style.

'Well, we'll see how well you do walking today,' I responded.

I regretted it instantly. Miles was reminded how tired he got and we were barely halfway around the rock. We saw Mike well ahead of us. He had found a fairly leafy tree and he sat under it waiting for us. Sweat came pouring from his forehead and nose.

He was amazed by the dramatic patterns in the sandstone and he pointed to the flocks of birds that lived in the little caves near the top. We paused and took in the overpowering enormity of this natural wonder. Miles revived and we got moving again. Just about five people had passed us in three hours. Miles must have thought it was strange and he kept bugging me with, 'Why are we walking around this mountain?'

Good question. I wanted to understand the dimension of it, see it close-up from all sides, read the stories of the Aboriginals that are connected with Uluru, and I wanted to pay a small tribute to their history, show my respect to their survival, their knowledge about nature, their strength against all hardships, in my own way, by walking. And I believed it would be a nice accomplishment for Miles. He'd be proud of his stamina and be able to say, 'I walked around this big rock.' So far so good. There were still two miles to be covered.

The scenery changed as we came around the rock, leaving behind the long backside of it. Carvings and stories about snakes accompanied us. One mile before we reached the car park Miles gave up. He had had enough. But somehow I didn't want Mike to carry him. I decided to talk Miles through to the bitter end. I made up stories about Sesame Street characters that were hiding in the bushes in front of us. It began to work. And, step by step, bush by bush, Ernie and Bert, Oscar and Big Bird helped us trot along. Closer and closer we got. All of a sudden we saw the parking area, and Miles ran to the campervan. Yes, there is always that bit of secret energy left in children that is released when their excitement awakens.

Next to our campervan we saw the long line of white people dressed in white shorts, white T-shirts and white socks, climbing up the crown jewel of Australia. They held on to a rope because it was a very steep ascent. Miles would have preferred to climb the rock instead of walking around it, he announced. He looked at me in disbelief when I reacted angrily. The Anangu ask every visitor to respect their sacred site and to refrain from climbing Uluru. They aren't banning people from it, rather they are asking them to make an educated choice. Their ancestors, the Mala men, used to climb Uluru. Now tourists are trampling over the sacred tracks of the Mala. I wonder how we would feel if herds of Aboriginal people trampled over the gravestones in our cemeteries or climbed the rooftops of our churches, maybe abseiling from the cross? Hundreds of people climb Uluru every day and many have accidents, a few have been fatal. The Aboriginal people mourn the injured and dead since they feel they have a responsibility for anyone who goes up there.

I don't understand why we always have to consume everything and anything. Here they are, the 'ants', as the Anangu say, consuming the rock, so that they can show off when they return home, saying they did it. Later on that day I saw a guy wearing a T-shirt that said 'I didn't climb Uluṟu.' I was consoled seeing someone considerate from my camp.

About ten miles from Uluṟu there is the Yulara resort, a village that consists of overpriced hotels, restaurants, a bank, a post office and the Ayers Rock Campground, and that is were we stayed. The best thing about the campground is that it has a pool and clean showers. We rewarded Miles with some pool time and a few dips into the ice water. At the age of five he had walked the base of the biggest monolith on earth. Wow! It was an accomplishment to be proud of.

Then we rushed to get ready for the famous sunset viewing. We drove twenty minutes out of Yulara to the designated area and were surprised by a huge row of people in cars or on their car rooftops waiting with their video or photographic cameras to capture the changing colors of the Rock. Although I wasn't quite sure if I liked the masses of people, I was still glad that we got one of the last spots in the first row. Miles was allowed to climb on the roof of the campervan and sit next to his Dad. He was ecstatic. Then he was allowed to use Dad's binoculars and do what everybody else out here was doing. Next to us was a young German couple on the rooftop of their beat–up VW camper. Miles talked some German to them. Proudly he told them that he had walked around that thing over there. He felt like a rock star.

Seeing Miles so excited I knew that by walking around it, the Rock had acquired a meaning for him. It wasn't just some odd red mountain that stuck out of the ground over there in the far distance. Miles, and we adults also, had gained a true feeling of the dimension of it.

Warayuki, Ngaltawata, Tjukatjapi, some names of the sites, the caves and crevices, came to my mind. There was so much to this grand place. From the onset of the sunset until the sun disappeared completely, the stone of the Rock changed from light brown over different shades of orange and ochre to deep, dark glooming copper, while the sky, at the same time, changed from light blue to dark blue mixed with violet to almost black. A movie of the purest colors. There is no imitation of the elements. Not the most advanced high-tech equipment is able to reproduce the clarity and intensity of these colors.

Uluru - the meeting place – filled my family with harmony after we had lived for an entire day through the changing moods of atmosphere and light at the foot of this great monolith.

18
Fiji
The Sunday Skirt
sulu vaka taga

'I got apple juice, mama! And they sang and clapped their hands. It was beautiful.' Miles's eyes rolled. His voice toppled.

'But what on earth are you wearing? You are in a skirt! Who gave you those clothes?' I wasn't sure if I should laugh or be concerned.

'Mama, I got apple juice in church. I love church,' Miles went on and on about this apple juice as if we never gave him anything sweet to drink. We are horrible parents really.

'Why are you wearing a skirt?' I was persistent.

Miles wore his *bula* shirt, a turquoise cotton shirt with a white floral design that we had bought for him in Nandi. He wouldn't stick out as much in a Fiji shirt, I thought at first. Nice try, I thought later. The effect of a boy with sun-bleached hair in a souvenir-type shirt was exactly the opposite. Today he also wore a black gabardine skirt that went way below his knees. A *sulu*, as the locals call it. It is worn on Sundays by the law-abiding Fijian Christian men. Now, try this. Go to your local gym, pick out the ten most muscular guys and roll their buttocks and thighs tightly in some black fabric. It is quite something to look at, believe me, Polynesian-Melanesian men on Sundays. Thank God their knees are covered.

'Who gave you the skirt?' I probed Miles and then he told me the story.

'After you and Dad left they took me down to the river and we all washed. They splashed me with the cold water and then this lady, Angelina's friend, gave me the skirt. She dressed me. We all went back up the hill to the churchhouse. We sang, well, I didn't but they did. And, and then I got apple juice. And then we played, and, and then you and Papa came back.'

By 'they' he meant the women of Abaca, a community in the highlands of Viti Levu, the largest of the Fijian islands. Its members generate their communal income by letting tourists stay with local families in the twenty *bures*, traditional Fijian cottages that are comfortably nestled in an emerald mountain valley like puppies in a green oversize beanbag chair.

Abaca lies about 7 miles off the coast from the town of Laukota, at the foot of the Koroyanitu National Heritage Park. Looking down from the summit of Castle Rock, which was about an hour and a half's climb, the village is nothing but a handful of scattered rooftops. If so far I had been quite disappointed by the deforestation of the island for the sake of sugar cane plantations, the rainforest around the base of Mount

Koroyanitu appeased me a little. Mike and I had taken our camcorder on the climb and we enjoyed the unobstructed views on the Yasawas and Mamanucas island groups. I peeked down to the village. Maybe I could see Miles. But we were too high above the village to make out any people. Even with eagle eyes we might not have seen them, since it was Sunday and everybody was attending church.

I hadn't thought about the possibility that Miles might be taken to mass, since I wasn't a practicing Christian anymore, but a wannabe Buddhist. That doesn't mean, of course, that I don't respect the choices people make about their beliefs, so I wasn't angered in any way when I found out that Miles had been taken to church. Far from it. I was amazed at how they integrated him like one of theirs, hardly knowing him.

The day before, a pickup truck had brought us to this sleepy village from a hotel in Laukota. We got off at the Abaca Visitor Center, a modest wooden building, light blue on the outside, with a desk and a couple of posters on the walls. The woman who runs the office had been informed of our arrival from people in Laukota. She opened a huge guest book and we entered our names and paid for the homestay. For a bed and three meals per day we were charged 30 Fiji dollars per person, which was $15 at the time. Miles could stay for free. The well-nourished Fijian woman explained to us that Joe and Angelina would be our hosts. The families in the village take turns hosting foreign travelers, she explained. As she spoke, another well-nourished woman, in a long skirt and with a hairstyle typical for ethnic Fijians, entered the building. Her frizzy hair was trimmed in a huge balloon shape around her head. She had a heart-warming smile on her face and she greeted us with a *bula, bula, vinaka,* which means as much as hello, hello, thank you.

Proudly she led us up to her home, a rectangular *bure.* The walls were made of bamboo stalks interwoven with palm leaves. The roof was high pitched and thatched. Traditionally there are no windows in a Fijian cottage. We entered through one of the low doors that are never locked and rarely shut. We dropped our backpacks in one of the corners of the room that was carpeted with mats made of a similar material to the walls. A flowery curtain separated two beds on the far side of the *bure* from the rest of the room.

Our *bure* wasn't one of the deluxe *bure*-style accommodations that the larger number of tourists who come to Fiji book with their travel agent. And we didn't have to dish out $1,453 per person per night. What was even nicer about our room was that it actually was a home of a Fijian family, and not some faceless, interchangeable resort cottage. Angelina told us that we would sleep in the two beds behind the curtain while they would sleep with friends, or family, or in the shack next door. I didn't quite understand what she said. Some Fijians are hard to understand when they speak English because it is broken English with a heavy accent. And when people make such an effort to speak your language while you can't speak theirs, I often nod as if understanding instead of prodding them with more and more questions.

The Fijian village of Abaca is like a daycare center, whose drop-off and pickup times are determined by sunrise and sunset. Pets, like pigs, horses, cats and dogs, are allowed. The grassy area in the village center and around the cottages is the playground. It is full of busy children chasing the animals, chasing each other, running in and out of the open doors, rolling around in the grass. There are no roads and no cars. The village is childproof.

Angelina is delighted to have a family with a small child as her guest. Miles is the star. The tourists who usually come to stay are young adults, but rarely do they travel with children. She walks around the hut and shows us her kitchen, a charcoal fire, sink with running water and wooden shelves for pots and pans, all in the open air.

'Wonderful,' Mike proclaimed. 'Looks just like my kitchen in Alaska.'

'Ah, you cook outside.' Angelina laughed, but didn't believe him.

She cooked cassava roots and rice and vegetables for us. Then we squatted in a circle on the mats around the set floor. Miles thought it was the greatest thing to eat while sitting on the ground. After lunch we met Angelina's husband Joe, a guy in black jeans and a blue T-shirt who looked too young to be her husband, but he was. We handed him the traditional gift, one pound of kava that we had bought in the market in Nandi. He received it well and announced that we all would get together later in the day, after dinner, and celebrate our welcoming the Fijian way.

Joe topped our pound of kava powder with some of his own and prepared a huge wooden bowl with the drink, while a few men and a crowd of elder women entered the *bure* and settled around the bowl cross-legged. The ground kava root was stuffed in a muslin cloth bag that looked like a sock without the heel. Water was filtered through the kava-filled sock, the kava ball was squeezed hard and the brew that dribbled into the bowl had a light brown complexion. Again and again the kava ball was immersed into the water and squeezed until the water finally looked like muddy liquid. Joe filled a coconut shell, clapped one time, said *bula* Mike, drank the kava in one gulp and clapped three more times. So that's how we had to do it, too. The shell went around, everyone greeted us with *bula* and we greeted back with *bula*.

I was a bit wary of drinking this disgusting looking and equally disgusting tasting stuff, but, of course, I was polite enough not to refuse. And it really is like eating olives; the more you drink from it and convince yourself that you like it, the more you actually do like it.

Two o'clock at night I awoke to the shaky voices of seventy-year-old women, still raising their old arms, lifting the coconut shell as if praying to a God, saying their '*buuula*'. I had been fast asleep behind the curtain for the last three hours. Now I pushed the curtain aside just enough so I could have a peek at the Fijian ladies who, without a doubt, were showing more stamina than me, the former party-until-dawn girl. I can't forgive myself for that. My husband had woken at the same time as me. He looked at me and shook his head in disbelief. The old Fijian women had shown us up.

I had to have another peek at them. Wrapped in woolen blankets, it gets pretty cold in the highlands once it's dark, they chatted quietly, smoked long, thin ladies' cigars and proceeded with emptying the kava bowl. My mouth was still a bit numb from the stuff. In fact, it reminded me of the one time that I chewed coca leaves walking the Inca trail in Peru. I was waiting for the effects that supposedly would make me run through the thin Andean air, instead I felt like I was sitting at my dentist's with my mouth wide open as he filled my teeth.

At five in the morning I woke again. This time I found them passed out on the floor, basically in the same spots where they had sat all evening, just that their bodies were stretched out, their heads rested on the bamboo mats. What a relief. They were human after all. And so they slept and snored off the kava.

You can't really talk about ethnic Fijians without mentioning cannibalism. The thought that cannibalism was practiced until the late 19th century is horrifying, and even more so are the stories about victims being forced to watch their body parts being eaten. The kava bowl in those days could have been made from the skull of a hated enemy. The famous travel writer Paul Theroux is, like many other foreigners who have come to Fiji, obsessed with its cannibalistic past. And I get the impression that he sees some of the traits still in the Fijians. I have a hard time associating any of this past with the soft-spoken, friendly highlanders who gave us their bed to sleep in, threw a welcome party for us, made us feel at home in their house and, last but not least, offered to watch our child when Mike and I told them about our plan to climb Castle Rock.

The thought of leaving my child in the care of people I didn't know and whose ancestors were cannibals is scary. Anything could have happened. That day in Abaca my stomach decided that I trusted these women and children to look after Miles. I just needed to make sure that Miles was okay with our decision. You can never tell a day in advance. But the morning when we put on our hiking gear he was already outside playing with Margarita, the three-year-old, super cute daughter of Joe and Angelina. When we walked up to him to remind him that we would be going on a three to four hour-hike he briefly waved bye-bye and swish, he was out of our eyesight, too involved in his play world to hold long conversations about babysitting arrangements.

The highlanders didn't eat my son for Sunday lunch, and I don't know whom to thank, the missionaries who came to the islands and abolished cannibalism or God. I don't know who, in the end, was the one who talked some sense into them. That Sunday night, however, my husband was captured by Joe and dragged to a secret meeting I wasn't allowed to go to. I stretched out on the bed waiting for Mike to come home and tell me what had happened. Hours later, as I was still alone, I was wondering how much kava Mike was forced to drink during the secret ceremony before they would finally slaughter him. He returned intoxicated but in one piece.

Life in the mountains of Viti Levu is refreshing because of the pristine green environment. Unfortunately, you get the impression that the few trees that are still there are hanging on like last soldiers in an already lost battle. Still, I felt so relaxed that I wished I could have stayed a couple of months. I have always been attracted by the life in tight knit, fairly self-sufficient communities, maybe because their social structure seems to encompass everyone's needs in a fair manner rather than just the needs of a few at the top.

Miles was so free up here. He had so many mothers and fathers, aunts and uncles, brothers and sisters. Most of his brothers and sisters spoke Fiji and no English.

Mike, Miles and I continued our highland tour to the village of Navala. This picture book traditional Fijian village of about 60 *bures* is set in the Nausori Highlands. We traveled by bus along the Kings Road to the town of Ba. From there two buses per day go up into the remote hills to Navala. We knew that we couldn't stay in the village itself because the chief wouldn't give us permission. So, the owner of a backpackers' hostel nearby took us into the village for a late afternoon stroll. We presented the chief with our gift and admired his well-kept community. About twenty guys in long brown pants and no tops were working on a steep roof construction. They greeted us with smiles. I wish I could have my neighbors get together and fix my roof after the next Florida hurricane. I wouldn't dare ask. Women sat together and chatted, others came back from the fields with cassava roots on the back of their donkeys, children were rolling around in the soft grass, then all of a sudden they stopped, stood up and stared at Miles, surprised by his presence in their village.

The river Ba trickled by below the village. Some women and children had gone down to the bridge to wash their clothes in the river. The mountain community appeared almost too peaceful to be part of this world. *Bula, Bula* we were welcomed by everybody, because we had brought a gift and paid a tribute to their chief, something like an entrance fee to visit Navala. The chatter and laughter that followed us as the chief showed us around was caused by the blond five-year-old who ran wild, stirring up the kids like chicken.

One day we went into the mountains on horses, took photos of the village from the bridge, then from further away, then from even further away. We couldn't get enough of the beauty. Then Miles got to harvest and plant cassava all morning. But the best thing of all was when we had to say farewell to the hostel owners. The bus came early in the morning to pick us up from under a tree outside of Navala; we hadn't been so sure if that would actually happen.

I had disliked our hosts from the very moment that we jumped off the back of the pickup truck that had given us a lift from the bus station to the hostel. A Fijian lady paced over the grass with fast, long steps, attacking me with her tight, almost manly embrace. She pressed wet kisses on both my cheeks. I quickly protected Miles as best as I could from a similar attack. She looked unusual for a Fijian woman. Her hair wasn't quite as frizzy. It was combed down toward the shoulders, not high up into the air. Her complexion was a little lighter, too. She could have passed for a mix between a Fijian and an Indian, but these things never happened on Fiji, so it seemed out of the question.

My mistrust was inflamed as she began to charge us way more for accommodation, meals and the horseback riding than the prices printed in our up-to-date guidebook. I disliked her so much that I refused to remember her name. She sat with us during every meal, but not because we all ate together, like at Angelina's. No. She took great pleasure in watching us. She made sure Miles overate since she charged him for his meals. He couldn't get away with eating only a third of what we ate, that would have been too embarrassing for her. Miles was tired of her and went into his stubborn mode whenever she appeared. He didn't react in the slightest to anything she said or did, which put us in an embarrassing situation. We constantly had to apologize for him. He is very tired, we told her, or it has been a long day for him. He has trouble eating when it is hot outside. He is not used to this kind of climate. He is very shy around people he doesn't know.

Over rice, cassava, and Fijian spinach, called *lolo*, we told her, quite unintentionally really, just to make conversation because she kept staring at our forks as they entered our mouths, that our next stop would be the island Nananu-i-Ra. This turned out to be a mistake. She knew now how to track us down and she found a good enough reason to do so.

In order to locate a family with a small child on the 350-hectare island of Nananu-i-Ra you don't need to have the skills of an FBI agent. You just need to call one of the three backpackers' places that are next to a row of private houses at the lower end where the island is so narrow that you can reach both beaches just by hopping over a small grassy hill. And that's what she did, the Navala woman, who became our fondest memory of the islands.

It happened in the morning of the third day on Nananu-i-Ra. Miles and I were walking to our small apartment after breakfast, when I was yelled at by some local who came running out of his hotel.

'Are you Stefanie?' he barked, visibly annoyed. 'Yes, you are', he answered his question himself while looking at Miles. 'I am fed up of having to deal with her phone calls,' he continued.

How come he knew my name? And who had been calling? I don't appreciate being yelled at by some stranger, certainly not at eight in the morning on a beautiful sunny island day. But I didn't want to yell back. So I asked him politely to explain the situation. The real culprit behind the yelling turned out to be the woman from Navala who had called several times, asking him to find me, claiming it was urgent. Why was she chasing us? I grinned. Maybe she had realized that she overcharged us. Maybe her Christian conscience told her that it was wrong to do so and she wanted to return the money to us. I asked if I could use his payphone. He agreed. When I called, nobody answered.

'I'll try to call her later,' I reassured the grump and left.

Miles and I spent the morning sitting on the beach making necklaces from tiny shells with holes in them. When I went back with the intention of calling her again, the unhappy hotel owner told me that she had rung three more times. Oh, boy. She trusted me as little as I trusted her. I asked Mike to call. She was home. And she accused my poor husband of having stolen her son's binoculars.

Her son had given us his binoculars when we went horse riding. Did we not return them? We certainly didn't steal them. What was she thinking? We might rob rich people, but not her and her friendly son. I felt sorry for him having to deal with her as a mother. Anyway, Mike checked his daypack and, sure enough, he found the binoculars that, in their black etui, almost looked identical to his camera. Since we had run out of change for the payphone, we left her a message that we would put the binoculars in a little box and send them to her from the post office in Rakiraki. The story goes on. Our suggestion wasn't good enough. She wanted us to travel back into the highlands to her place. So she continued to pester the hotel owner with three more phone calls until it was him who tracked us down at the beach and began to accuse us of stealing. He demanded the binoculars in front of all the other tourists present on the island. He even stretched out his open hand. By God, we were really popular on the island now. His hand, however, remained empty.

People aren't all the same. Wherever you go you met the good and the bad and that's no extraordinary revelation. Therefore, we continued loving the company of the ethnic Fijians, and also of the Indo-Fijians, of which we met fewer, although the population of Fiji is almost equally divided between the two groups.

For now, it was time to change the scenery and leave the densely populated coastal areas of Viti Levu and to seek some adventure on the satellite islands of Vanua Levu and Taveuni. But before we left we did go to the post office, lest Miles should think that his parents were ruthless thieves.

19

Ratatouellie [Ratatui], Ratatouellie [Ratatui]

The name of the French eggplant and zucchini dish sounds identical to the chorus of a song that I heard over and over again here on Fiji, with the result that until the day I die I will wrongly associate eggplants and zucchini with the South Pacific. Fijians love to double their words or syllables. Why, I don't know. Towns are called Rakiraki and Savusavu. Other examples are kava kava or the catchy song ratatui, ratatui.

Miles had finished his meal and he got up to sit with a group of Fijian musicians around the kava bowl. Mike and I enjoyed the romantic atmosphere of the intimate beach restaurant in the town of Matei on Taveuni island. Hibiscus flowers and candles decorated our and the other four tables. A faint but deliciously sweet barbecue smell came from the plundered buffet in front of us. Not much was left of the *lovo*, the traditional Fijian food wrapped in banana leaves and cooked in an earth oven. Just a few pieces of meat, some banana cake and papaya.

Full of wonder, our son was entertained by ethnic Fijian folk music. I took the opportunity to take my husband's hand. I squeezed it tight and said, 'I think I'll go for seconds.'

I got up discreetly. Mike leaned back and listened to the Fijian music. Earlier on we had participated in a *meke*, a traditional dance performance, and danced with the Fijian locals in their flowery costumes. The steps were easy, surprisingly similar to Latin American *merengue*.

I guess if it wasn't for the hibiscus flower the Fijians wouldn't know what to print on their dresses and shirts. I do love the flower, it's just that it's everywhere on these Pacific islands. I have gone as far as to stick the flowers behind my ear in my hair. It looks sexy, and I would wear it all the time if it wasn't for the ants that love the flowers as much as everyone else. One or two insects always manage to hide somehow in the flower, then they crawl into your hair, into your ear, ratatui, ratatui, …

I never pushed Miles to shake hands with people or talk with people who are strangers to him. When Miles gets up on his own account and walks over to a group of people he has never met before then there must be something about these people, their gestures, their faces, their voices that make him feel comfortable and safe. After three weeks on Fiji Miles was familiar with the kava drinking ceremonies. Sitting cross-legged around a kava bowl with us was something he had done several times now. He felt special sitting with us and other adults. He was also familiar with the music, the rhythmic sounds of the

Fijian guitar and ukelele and the high-pitched voices of the Fijian men, ratatui, ratatui, …

There is a rather brutal fable behind the kava that says that several hundreds years ago the King of Toga visited an island plagued by famine. Desperate to offer something to the king, a woman cooked her baby, wrapped it in leaves and sacrificed it to the king. The king sensed that it wouldn't be right to eat the baby. He ordered a princely burial. And out of the grave grew the kava plant that alleviated all hunger. Today, in Fiji, kava drinking is important to community gatherings and the welcoming of guests, ratatui, ratatui, …

The first time that Miles surprised us with his attraction to the kava drinking ceremony was one morning when we had breakfast at a small resort in Savusavu on Vanua Levu. He sat at the table in the resort's restaurant with a glass of milk in front of him. All of a sudden I saw and heard him clap his hands once, lift up the glass of milk, chuck it down in one go and clap his hands three times to finish the event. Mike and I burst out in laughter.

'*Bula*, Miley,' I said. 'Welcome to Fiji! Ratatui, ratatui…'

On the same day, when we ordered our dinner and the waiter asked him what he wanted to drink, he blurted out, 'Kava kava.'

Mike and I looked at each other and shrugged our shoulders. Until then he had refused to drink, the not very appetizing looking drink and I don't really blame him. The Fijian waiter thought the whole situation was quite amusing and he asked the three Fijian men who sat in the restaurant's corner playing folk music if Miles could join them for a shell of kava. Their faces lit up and they embraced Miles in their circle around the kava bowl. They clapped and shouted *bula*, then they played a song for Miles extra loud, RATATUI, RATATUI …

A traveler from Britain had joined us at our table. He couldn't believe that Miles would go and sit with these men all by himself. 'Your boy isn't shy, is he!' he stated rather than asked.

'Funny that you say that,' I commented. 'He can be very shy. Sometimes it's hard for me to tell if he is stubborn or shy, but certain people he simply ignores. He walks past them as if they were air, even while they are still talking to him. It is embarrassing. I ask him to at least be polite. But with all this traveling he is fed up with saying his name ten times over and telling people where he comes from. Sometimes he says he comes from Germany, sometimes he comes from England. The choice is arbitrary, as far as I can tell. But, yes, you are right, on most occasions he isn't shy at all. He certainly doesn't make any distinctions with respect to the origin or language of the people.'

'He seems pretty comfortable over there,' the British guy remarked.

'Yes. It's because those guys don't ask him questions, but show him something new. He watches, he feels integrated and then later he talks. I better get him, though. He just had his second bowl of kava. I can't believe he is drinking this muddy river water with driftwood aroma.'

I knew that the narcotic effect of one or two kava bowls is not much stronger than the effect of several cups of black tea. The Fijians give kava to their children. It makes them sleep well, they say. With Miles it was hard to tell the difference. He slept for 12 hours after his dinner with kava, but that's not unusual.

A few days later some Melbourne girls with their transvestite cook hung out at the resort bar and invited us to a party at their house. Fiji is full of Australian landowners, businessmen and tourists. You can't escape them. Since we didn't have anything better to do that evening we went to see them. The party took place at a private villa about eight miles east of Savusavu. It is expensive to take a taxi all the way so we hooked up with one of the local real estate agents who showed us some land for sale in first class locations near the Australians' house. We then mentioned, as if by chance, the party throwers' names, which immediately rang a bell with the real estate agent, and it didn't surprise us. To be honest, we had counted on it. He knew them very well and he offered to drop us off at their house.

Australians have a rational love for children. They produce plenty and then arrange activities for them so the kids don't get bored. Fijians have an irrational love for children. They hug, kiss and squeeze them, and they don't separate them from their daily routines. Fijian children have few toys, but they have the company of plenty of relatives, herds of other children, animals and nature.

Miles played for a while with the Australian kids in the sand, but as soon as he saw the Fijian servants and gardeners with their families settle around the kava bowl he chose to abandon his Australian mates. Don't try to tell me that he was already addicted to kava. I'll tell you what he was addicted to. It was the attention he got from the Fijians. He settled on the bamboo mat, he crossed his legs, that must have reminded him of preschool, and there he sat for the reminder of the evening listening to the clapping, the bula, the songs, and the ukelele.

Fijian mamas were suckling their babies and rocking them to the rhythm of the music.

We were lucky to get a lift back into town from one of the guests. There was no way the owners of the exclusive resort next door would have let us stay for the night. Not that we had a spare 1,500 Fijian dollars for a garden *bure*, but children under the age of 12 aren't accepted. The luxury resort is no exception. Most resorts that overcharge for exclusivity and decadence hate to see children on their premises.

Quite truthfully, I understand the mentality of people who desire to vacation in a childfree zone very well. It had been such a nightmare to travel with Miles on Fiji, Mike and I didn't know what to do. He nagged and whined and whined and nagged. But there is a local remedy. We began to feed him kava, bowl after bowl, so that he became drowsy and lethargic by midday, and he would stare into the ocean for the rest of the afternoon not saying a single word, until he finally passed out and there was silence.

20

About the Man,
Who Lived in a Coconut

There is a legend of the "Dreamland of the West", Nananu-i-Ra, which says that once upon a time there was a girl called Adi from the tribes of Viti Levu who fell in love with a young chief from the tribes of Bua. Unfortunately, the tribes of Bua and the tribes of Viti Levu weren't friendly, and both fathers rejected the relationship. The lovers, however, continued to see each other secretly on the island of Nananu-i-Ra, the beautiful "Dreamland of the West". Thus goes the legend of old Fiji.

A traveler's story of new Fiji tells us about a miserable old European lady who walked out on the pier of Nananu-i-Ra one morning. When she met a young tourist boy she stopped briskly, looked at his face and said, 'Oh, Lord. What are you doing here in the Dreamland of the West? You should be in school!'

Then she looked up at his parents reproachfully, and her face grimaced.

'Why is your son not in school? He wants to learn and be with his friends. What could he possible learn here? Fiji is boring.'

She looked down at the boy, her white makeup gleaming in the tropical sun, and said with real emotion, 'Poor thing. You must be so bored.'

She couldn't have enjoyed the natural beauty of Nananu-i-Ra. She gave the impression that she was forced to be there.

Do you argue with this kind of person? No, you don't. I was steaming. Jealous old cow. But there was another reason why I reacted so defensively. We had studied the ABCs in Australia, but other than that I hadn't done anything academic with Miles. We had been too busy in Fiji traveling from island to island, going to the beach, collecting shells and diving. Miles had spent a lot of time playing with the local children.

And after Nananu-i-Ra there was Taveuni. Mike had found us a luxurious house to stay in on the northern tip of the island. One day after we arrived he strolled along the one and only street that runs through Matei and he met a middle-aged local who was the caretaker of the beach house that belonged to an American doctor. Better than me at connecting with people and negotiating astonishing deals, Mike persuaded the man to rent the doctor's house to us. The doctor was far away in the States, whereas we were here and willing to turn the caretaker into a rich man for the next ten days.

It was quite a change to move from our tent into this tasteful wooden home where we had separate rooms and baths.

We square-danced over the large verandah with ocean view hesitantly, still not quite believing our shameless luck. We skipped down the steep rocky steps that lead onto something you could call our own private beach. And the caretaker, whose popularity rose steadily over the next week, threw beer party after beer party.

On the doctor's verandah we would play games. Mike and Miles would go swimming about four times a day. They would see cool things like an octopus and sea snakes. And then a Swiss woman with a young boy Miles's age arrived in town. The mother was the only single mom I have ever met traveling with her child. Both of them had been to Australia, where they had worked together on an organic farm. The boy was multilingual and very active. He and Miles got along fine.

The next stop for us was going to be Suva. We would take a flight across the Koro Sea. The mother and son team was heading in the same direction just a day later. We arranged to meet at a lodge near the Colo-I-Suva Forest Park, some seven miles north of Suva.

Suva can be a hectic city. It is the bazaar of Fiji's main island. Indo-Fijian shops lean side-by-side, ethnic Fijian shops are few and far between. The Indo-Fijians, the descendents of indentured workers brought from India by the British, live mainly in the cities of Nandi and Suva.

Generally, bargain and souvenir shopping with a child is a complete nightmare, especially in the narrow, busy shops of Suva where I had a hard time looking after Miles. Whenever I let go of his hand he ran away and sat himself on the doorstep of the shop an inch away from the enormous speaker boxes. Since Hindu and Muslim shopkeepers alike love to crank up their stereos just to be louder than the shop next door, Miles's ears sure got a sound beating. What's worse is that each time I was afraid someone would pass by and snatch him away in the second I wasn't looking. After a few hours we had bought a kava bowl, bottles of noni juice, two new daypacks and a pair of shoes for Miles. Miles was still with us and he still seemed to be able to hear us.

Our quiet enclave was only a short bus ride away. As we entered the lodge Miles ran into his Swiss friend. He and his mom had just arrived. We happened to share the same room. The private rooms were full, so we were sleeping in a dorm. Dorm accommodation is quite common on Fiji. It is the Australian influence. Aussies love dorms. I wouldn't know what the fun of it is. We were lucky in that the lodge owner had some mixed gender dorms, something that isn't always the case. But even if he hadn't, come afternoon he was so drunk that he couldn't have told a man from a woman anyway.

The great advantage of drunks, though, is that they do for you whatever you ask. Everything is possible. How about free lemonade for the kids? *Sure, no problem.* How about taking the boys out on the lake in the old boat? *Sure, no problem.* How about asking the cook if he could prepare the fish that they caught for their dinner? *Whaaaat? They want to eat what they caught?* Yes. *Okay then. No problem.* We loved it at the lodge.

All in all the area around Suva is damp and green. It rains almost every day of the year. That's why most tourists never come to Suva. Mike, Miles and I visited the Colo-I-Suva Forest Park on two days for short hikes. One day we walked along the Falls Trail past the Waisila Falls to some natural swimming pools with rope swings. Resting from the in parts quite slippery and steep walk we watched the local adolescent boys climbing up a huge rock that towered above one of the swimming holes.

The rope, whose end dangled about 15 feet above the water's surface, was passed to the youngster who stood on the highest spot. He would swing and encourage someone else to jump on the rope with him, and maybe they would cheer a third one on, swing, and then all together dive into the water. The sport was a manly, boisterous one. The one who dared the most was cheered on; he was the hero.

'I want to do it.' Miles said out of the blue.

'No. I don't think so.' I replied before I realized what he had said.

Nobody was listening to me. My husband must have waited for this opportunity. He grabbed Miles's hand and rushed up to the top of the lower rock where most of the guys stood waiting for their go. Even they stared in disbelief. I was scared. Miles could barely swim. What if ... I decided against closing my eyes. A tall and skinny 15-year-old handed Mike the rope. Miles sat on his arm. One, two, three, jump ... this was crazy. A few seconds later, their heads popped out of the freezing water. Mike was paddling with one arm and supporting my smiling boy with his other arm. The locals cheered and shouted in their language. Whatever it was that they said, the chorus encouraged Miles and Mike to have a second go. I knew when it came to taking risks Miles's threshold was low, although that's pretty normal for most children given that they have no idea of what could happen. Mike's threshold, however, was unusually low for an adult. Sometimes I admire it, at all times I live with it.

The last highlight on our Fiji tour was an Australian owned, low-key, backpackers' resort. Not very authentic Fijian, but an absolute fun place for young people and families with children. Here is a piece of advice, however, if you like what you read and you want to spend your next vacation here: Hurry! Global warming experts predict that a large part of Southern Viti Levu will disappear within the next 30 years, due to sea water levels rising, which in turn causes coastal areas to flood and erosion to occur.

We settled comfortably into our yellow and purple beach cottage, a double room with wooden flooring and mosquito nets. The bathrooms for everyone who lived in the cottages and in the dorms were communal. Miles always took showers with Mike. One evening, to the amusement of all the other guys who were brushing their teeth or taking showers, Miles announced loud and clear, 'You have a big one and I have a small one.' Now that's why you travel with children!

This time we were all-inclusive, with tea and scones British style in the afternoons. Four meals are great for children who are always hungry. Between hunting sea snakes, another one of Mike's ventures, and beachcombing for shells, Miles and I would gather with other tourists around the Fijian gardener who demonstrated how to weave hats, baskets and Christmas tree decoration out of palm leaves.

It didn't take me long to realize that the average age of the British, Scottish and Australians who stayed at the resort was not older than 25. All the more it surprised me that everyone paid so much attention to Miles. When I was in my twenties, children annoyed the hell out of me. All day long there was somebody who wanted to do something with Miles. 'Why don't you go and flirt with the girl in the skimpy bikini instead, or get yourself a beer and swing in the hammock?' I was thinking when guy after guy, girl after girl came to baby-sit. I never complained, though.

A young American entrepreneur called Parker became Miles's buddy. The two were inseparable. Parker played Tarzan and came flying off coconut palm trees. He taught Miles how to fly from tree trunks over several feet of grass. He constructed a boat out of sand in which Miles could sit and be the captain. Parker danced with Miles on the restaurant's tables. He protected Miles from the embraces of all the young girls who thought Miles was so cute. Parker unwrapped the straws and stuck them in Miles's juice boxes, he caught huge crabs and he found a coconut with a little man inside.

One evening after dinner the man in the coconut spoke to Miles and Miles spoke back to him. Everyone was holding his breath. Nobody around the table of 12 wanted to spoil the game. Parker was a stand-up comedian. He changed his voice and, while he pressed the coconut to one of Miles's ears, he whispered into the other one. Miles told the man every little detail about the world trip, he told him his age, and asked him to come outside. The little man said that maybe tomorrow he would come out of the coconut, but it was too late now and Miles needed to go to bed.

'Keep me and put me in front of the door of your cottage. Goodnight, Miles.'

'Goodnight, little man,' Miles whispered.

He took the coconut, stood up and asked me to take him to bed. Mike got up in my place and walked him to the cottage. As soon as both of them were out of sight the girls at the table attacked Parker.

'Didn't you see how he knocked at the coconut for the man to come out. He believed every word you said. He'll be waiting tomorrow and nothing will happen,' one of the girls said with a teary voice.

Parker felt guilty. I laughed. Miles had tricked all of them. He loved to act and, for the entire time of the game, he had acted as if he believed in the little man. And tomorrow morning he would step outside his cottage and hold the coconut against his ear and mom would whisper in the other ear, 'Pack up your stuff. It's time to leave Fiji.'

21

Costa Rica
Machetes 'r' us

He's going to chop his right foot off. It went through my head
as I watched Gerardo play around with this huge knife that was
the length of an adult's arm. The Costa Ricans pronounce it
maschet-te. It's Spanish for lawn mower, tree branch cutter, leaf
chopper, snake killer, and can opener. It also opens coconuts,
and that's the main reason why Gerardo runs around with it.

Gerardo is four years old and the *maschet-te* reaches up to his
shoulders, the pointed end touching the ground. That's why,
when he jogs with it, it looks like any minute his foot will come
flying at you. I watched him climb up an old wooden ladder
with the knife in hand and I wished I could be as relaxed about
it as his mother, who fed the horses next to the coconut tree
Gerardo was climbing. Chop, chop, bang. The green coconut,

or *pipa*, fell on the ground and Gerardo picked it up. Then he asked his mother to cut the top part open so that he could drink the clear coconut water from it.

His mom went into the house to get a couple of straws and Gerardo was asked to get another *pipa* for Miles. When I had offered Miles coconut water the first time he had refused to even try. After seven days in Costa Rica it became his favorite drink. The explanation is straightforward. Gerardo, who he imitates, drinks about seven or eight *pipas* every day with the passion of a thirsty boy.

Fiji – United States – Costa Rica. We gained a day flying over the date line, a day we could have happily done without because we spent it on planes and in airports. Our flight from Nandi left four hours late. We missed connecting flight after connecting flight down to Costa Rica. It took us days to even get close to Central America. Finally we landed in the Central Valley at the Juan Santamaría Airport, twenty minutes outside of San José, and I felt home. I had tears in my eyes, some sort of a belated homesickness mixed with the melancholy of an aging person who realizes how quickly time flies by. It was almost six years ago that I had left Costa Rica. After all this time I returned, able to show the country that I love to my son and husband. I sobbed to myself. It was a happy sort of sobbing that makes you think of people who listen to opera music and can't help it but cry.

We stayed the night in San José. I forgot how polluted the city was. Fumes from cars that would be illegal to drive in our cities blacken your hands from whatever you touch in the streets, the switch at the pedestrian light, the T-shirts that are sold, and the fruit. Starved from the trip we entered a *soda*, a basic Costa Rican restaurant comparable to a diner in the States, and after the first bite of my dinner I remembered how greasy the food was. Later, Miles escaped his death by about an inch when a violent taxi driver, no rarity in Latin America, raced toward him as he was crossing the road. Fresh off the plane, San José was too much to be taken in for long. We decided to have a very early night.

The next morning we woke with the plan to take the bus to the Caribbean village of Puerto Viejo. Once a sleepy village of turtle hunters and cocoa farmers, today a surfer's, backpackers', and environmentalist's haven. I was looking forward to seeing the few good friends that I still had in the village and who hadn't met my family yet. As we bought our bus tickets I was told that we could only travel as far as the Caribbean port of Limón. In Limón, we had to change buses. Hopefully there would be a bus to Puerto Viejo, since the Caribbean rainy season had brought more buckets of rain than usual and had flooded the streets. Entire bridges had disappeared. Would we make it to Puerto Viejo? There was no guarantee. There never is in Costa Rica.

For Mike and Miles, an introduction to the chaotic life of the Caribbean lowlands came fast. The bus, with more people in it that it should have had, swerved around enormous potholes halfway down the coast to Puerto Viejo. Potholes, a common feature of Costa Rican roads, remind me of a radio competition that ran one Christmas. The person who could find the largest pothole, in diameter and depth, would win a prize. The winning entry was a pothole you could have made a chair disappear in. It's good news that at least the Costa Ricans laugh about their government's inefficiency.

The road we drove on was close enough to the beach that you could see the waves break through a row of palm trees. It is an attractive ride, besides the swells of tropical heat that enter the bus as soon as it stops to let locals on or off.

All of a sudden the bus came to a halt. We were told to get off, all of us with our luggage. There was no town, no gas station just road. The tall Costa Rican who had sat next to Mike and was now getting up mumbled something in English about the bridge being down. The river had flooded the road in front of us. The only way to cross was by foot along the beachfront, where the water wasn't as deep. Still, we would have to wade through knee-high waters to the other side. Everyone grabbed his small bundle, except for us. We had heavy backpacks and additional daypacks, including Miles, who carried seven pounds of his belongings. There was only one other tourist on the bus. He was lucky enough to have had his backpack stolen out of the outer luggage compartment in San José. A few Costa Ricans saw it happen. They stirred up the crowd at the bus terminal by talking fast and loud, throwing their arms in the air. But nobody actually did anything. I believe that the only reason why this backpack-less tourist continued his journey was to show travelers like us how idiotic it is to travel heavily loaded.

We ached and cursed as we followed the cultural mix of people we shared the bus with, a mix that was typical for the Caribbean coast. Afro-Caribbeans, tall, with fancy hairstyles, colorful hairclips or dreadlocks, peacocked behind *Ticas*, Costa Rican women of Indian and Spanish descent, who wore clothes far too tight, too elegant in cut, and too synthetic for the 95 degree humidity and the muddy occasion. The Bribri Indians were the smallest people of the busload. Quietly they followed everyone else, the poorly moustachioed men wearing greasy hair and black rubber boots. Sensible, I thought. I had bought Wellington boots in San José in one of those awkward stores next to the *mercado central* that sells women's lingerie, shoes and ice cream. I guess there is no compelling economic argument that speaks against the unusual compilation of stock.

I took my sandals off and put my boots on then I helped Miles into his. We wasted some time and were behind everyone else. Miles determined our pace as we hastened down to the beach. His feet sunk into the deep mud. He got stuck and I had to take his rubber boots off and let him walk on bare feet. After we had made it through the river, I had to change Miles into dry clothes and clean his feet just good enough so that he could put his boots back on. I was nervous, eager to catch up with Mike and the rest, because I knew the bus on the other side of the river wouldn't wait for us. After Mike had tossed his backpack in the bus he came running toward us to give us a hand. I was sweating and the straps of my daypack cut into my shoulder. Welcome back to Costa Rica. What was it that had made me think this was a wonderful country to live in?

Bocas del Toro lends itself to being an attractive weekend getaway for people in Puerto Viejo. So we took a holiday from our holiday and boated from island to island exploring the Panamanian archipelago that borders to the South of Costa Rica. I noticed how tourism had really picked up on the main islands since I had been there last. I had to say the same for Puerto Viejo, despite its unglamorous reputation as a tourist destination.

Admittedly, the town of Puerto Viejo would profit from a massive cleanup and a few hundred gallons of glossy deluxe paint. The villagers rely far too much on the population of vultures that crown the palm trees during the day and fish for eatable garbage in the stinking open drains and along the roads during the dark. But even those greedy birds cannot keep up.

Costa Rican mainstream tourism is directed away from the Talamanca coast. A trademark of Cahuita and Puerto Viejo are the ex hippies, boozers, druggies and women who consume Rastas. So everyone travels to the Pacific Coast, to overpopulated Jaco and Quepos, or to the dried-out, shriveled up Guanacaste region. But that's quite all right with me. I hope it doesn't change.

The splendor of the Talamanca region is its lush virgin forests, its humid climate and its colorful folklore. It serves as a hideaway for the devout nature lovers and individualists among the locals and expats, the ones that you rarely see in town because they lead a quiet life in their healthy enclaves in the green hills.

My dream is to own a small nature retreat for my family. Therefore, upon returning from Panama, we bought an acre of land from a friend and tied ourselves to Costa Rica as proud landowners. To be exact, we bought an acre of thick, impenetrable jungle.

In rural Caribbean Costa Rica you measure distances in bicycle minutes. Our diamond-shaped property is a twenty-minute bike ride out of town, a five-minute bike ride from an unspoiled beach, and a two-minute bike ride to our next-door neighbor, who happens to have electricity.

I think Miles was the only five-year-old child in town who wasn't able to ride a bike. It is irrelevant if the kids own bicycles or not. By the time they are three-and-a-half they know how to manipulate a bike and, when they turn four, they are allowed to pedal on their own to the shops and to the beach. It doesn't sound as dangerous as it actually is, but since the old village of farmers and fishermen converted into a center for tourism, the main street that runs through the village was tarmaced. Local macho men in cars and Italian residents on four-wheelers behave like bulls on steroids and race up and down the tarmac making the otherwise tranquil town unsafe for stray dogs and kids on bikes.

Over much of the coming weeks we spent our time away from the town's action on the property. We cleared the land with the help of local workers. They were the first to step into the jungle and chop it down with machetes. Mike and I followed, digging out roots of banana trees and heliconias, raking the forever falling leaves and cutting down worthless trees and shrubs that the laborers thought we might want to keep. The jungle had grown over a former cocoa plantation. The cocoa trees, although still standing, were sick. That's why the farm had been given up some 25 years ago. We cut all of the cocoa trees but one. Another type of tree that we eliminated from the property is one whose long dark spines make you feel uneasy. These spines are filled with a juice that blinds you should it get in your eye. Reason enough for Mike to protect his eyes with a scuba diving mask when he cut them down. The trees' fall produced a noise as if they were shot with a gun, then they crashed to the ground.

The tropical rainforest in Costa Rica is a magical place for children and adults alike but not entirely without dangers. *Terciopelos*, as they call them in Costa Rica, are aggressive deadly snakes that will attack you. Pit vipers sit quietly in trees and sleep, but when woken they move fast and bite. Not many mortals dance as lightly footed through the forest as native Roberto. I swear he smells the reptiles and insects around him. With great caution he picked up a sleeping pit viper and put it on another tree just to confuse it. We watched and I wondered how his mother had coped with him and this peculiar hobby of his, when he was a child. Then again, whatever you grow up with, that's what normality means for you. You don't know any different. What else would you compare it with? If you grow up with snakes their presence is normal for you. That doesn't protect you entirely from accidents, but you learn how to behave around them. Just like we learn the laws of cosmopolitan cities with their traffic and crime; and we don't think anything of it. Someone who grew up in the jungle might find cities frightening. For instance, Roberto told me that on his first trip to Europe he was in his twenties and the big city traffic and the underground trains scared him so much that he stayed in his room for weeks.

It was 6:30 in the morning. I jumped on my bike to get fresh bread and juices from the bakery. Roberto passed on his bike. I bet he had been up since 5 a.m. People get up early in the tropics to appreciate the cool morning air.

After breakfast Mike, Miles and I left our concrete *cabina* to work on the land. Miley sat on my handle bar while Mike was carrying a chainsaw on his bike. We rode along the tarmac road that runs parallel to the beach until it turns left and leaves the coast to go inland. That's where we turned right and carried on along a broad gravel road that used to be an airstrip maintained by the Loffland Oil Company. The company came to the Talamanca coast in the early '50s drilling for the precious natural resource, oil. Fortunately, the oil they found wasn't commercial enough and the company left. For a number of years private planes landed on the airstrip. Today, houses line the gravel runway. An uneven dirt path to the right leads first closer to the beach and then it winds itself into the forest. As we came around a sharp corner we nearly ran into our German neighbor, his *Tica* wife and their three dogs. The skinny young man was delighted to see us and to get us involved in Puerto Viejo politics.

'What are you going to do?' he asked. 'Or have you not heard?'

We had heard, but everyone's story was different.

'I came here five years ago to have my peace and quiet.' His voice was starting to acquire an edge. 'If they come I will pack my bags and go to Osa, the last place in Costa Rica where it is still nice.'

I shrugged my shoulders. Whatever everyone was talking about, it would take centuries to materialize. This was Central America.

'Well, we will see,' I mumbled irrelevantly.

'We held meetings in town to protest against the plan of the ICT,' he continued. 'They want to build a marina out here where we are. This will be the end of it for all of us out here. The animals will move further inland. ICT hasn't got local sensibility. I am telling you, I will pack my bags. Osa, I say to my wife. The only place left is Osa.'

His wife smiled at him. She must have heard his angry speech numerous times before.

'I understand,' I said. 'I am sorry, but we have to move on. We are meeting with our workers in five minutes, and we have to get started on the land before it gets too hot.'

'Your land is starting to look nice. But when the ICT comes to develop this area, I will go to Osa,' he rattled on while we waved good-bye.

Sitting high up on the saddle my face got caught in some cobwebs. Spiders with long orange bodies and athletic legs spin them across the path during the night. We arrived, flung our bikes on the ground, and quietly paced the cleared land. I savor the sensations delivered to my eyes and ears when I am in the jungle. Huge brown leaves swayed to the ground as if it was fall. We heard a dark half roar, half gurgle in the distance. The call of a howler monkey. Maybe it sensed our presence and warned its relatives.

Miles climbed a small tree with hardly any leaves. It was his designated place while we worked. From up there he felt in control. He watched us work and played pirate until he thought about helping us for a while. I let him rake the areas that are exposed to the sun where snakes don't like to hang out. We all wore rubber boots despite the heat and I also wore gloves to pick up debris and pull out roots. Every so often a neon turquoise butterfly the size of both my hands would gracefully glide through the trees across the land. Each of us would stop working and lift our heads up to follow it with our eyes. It is the morpho butterfly, the largest butterfly there is.

Later, Mike called us and pointed out a sloth in the top of a large tree. The bear look alike with arms far too long and a head that shrunk in the wash, sat motionless for quite some time before we witnessed one of those rare sloth moments. The animal lowered itself down from the tree to pee on the ground and then climb up another tree. Miles watched the fascinating ceremony that lasted almost one hour.

By lunchtime Miles would get bored. Typically we had tuna fish sandwiches and soda with the workers, I translated some of my husband's jokes into Spanish and then I left them for two more hours of chopping and sign language while Miles and I went for a dip in the ocean.

Although our place was by far no farm, I do love the Spanish expression '*voy a la finca*,' 'I am going to my farm,' and so I used it all the time. It sounds rural, the appropriate thing to say since we exercised hard physical labor. One day I was by myself on the *finca* because Mike had to round up materials and helpers for the construction of the fence. Actually, I was with Miles and one local guy. Half an hour into the work I heard the guy, whose name is Juan, scream. I tried to find Juan but there were too many trees that obstructed my view. Eventually, he came galloping toward we with a broad smile on his face as if he had just eaten a super size Big Mac and his mouth was still over-stretched. In his hand he held a long green snake.

'It fell out of the tree and on my back,' he said. Luckily it wasn't a poisonous snake. Then, he announced proudly, 'I am going to kill it.'

Never had I seen anyone so delighted about killing something. His fingers pressed the snake's jaws together. The instant they let loose, the blade of his machete shot down and separated the snake's head from its body.

'Aaaaaaahhhh.' A loud scream silenced the jungle.

'Where is Miles?' I yelled, overcome by a sudden fright.
Juan didn't hear me. Intoxicated he stared at the dead snake and began to dance.

'Juan, where is Miles, goddamnit?' this time I screamed in his ear.

There was no need, really. Everybody in Costa Rica seemed to have better hearing than me. Maybe my ears had been deafened by the noises of civilization. Juan looked up at me and darted to the creek.

'He is at the bridge,' he shouted.

He must have heard some splashing in the water. I reached the bridge after a sprint that would have qualified me for the Olympics. Miles stood in the creek crying. He had sneaked off to play fisherman at the wooden bridge without railings and he had lost his balance. The water reached up to his belly button. There must be snakes in the water, I assumed, panic stricken. But Juan had already grabbed his arm and he was now pulling him up.

Our saga of snake incidents reached its climax the following day. About a five-minutes bicycle ride past our *finca* there lives a real farmer. Regularly, he herds his white cows with funny looking bumps on their backs along the far side of the *finca*, and then over the bridge. Carlos always smiles, displaying two perfect rows of white teeth. Today the cheerful and friendly man looked saddened. The string that functions as a belt and holds up his old and gray suit pants looked sad, too. What was the problem? Mike and I approached him. After we greeted each other he said, '*Cam with me. A boa killed my caaf this manin. I had to kill them boa. Chop it into pieces. But too late. Them caaf is dead now. Falla me.*'

I took Miles by his hand and we followed Carlos. I wasn't quite sure if the massacre of a dead calf and a dead snake was the right thing for Miles to see. But he had heard Carlos speak and he was as curious as we were. God knows what Carlos really meant. I couldn't imagine a snake killing a calf. For what reason? Calves don't attack snakes and snakes only kill their prey. Can you picture a snake swallowing a calf? We carefully climbed through the barbed wire fence and walked across the meadow to where a group of cows gathered. There it was, a terrible sight. The eight feet long boa, a massive beast, had wrapped itself around the calf's neck. An occurrence so unusual and mysterious that nobody in town believed us.

Miles's eyes grew huge and his mouth opened. He was amazed more than terrified. He is a kid that's difficult to scare. Carlos had tears in his eyes. The herd is his soul. There was no consoling him. We walked back in silence. Mike and I both thought the same. Reassuring to know that we have monster boas living with us on and around the land that we bought. Maybe the purchase of a piece of jungle in the jungle was an irresponsible move that we would regret one day. Maybe we are too urbanized to cope with wildlife. Maybe we should have bought a pumpkin farm in the Midwest instead, I thought while I painted fence posts later on that morning. I was wary that any minute a snake might dip into my paint pot. Mike and Juan had set seventy concrete fence posts around our property. Miles helped me paint them green. And while I painted seventy posts, two coats each, I had the time to think about an awful lot of things.

In the afternoon Mike and I read books on our small verandah. Miles was at the beach with Gerardo, his sister Nadine and his mother. I sat in a white plastic chair next to Mike, who swung in a hammock. All of a sudden Mike heard a light tapping sound. He looked on the table next to me. Two inches from where I had placed my elbow a crab spider the size of a dinner plate had landed. I glanced at it, jumped up in total hysterics, crashed into our bicycles, which fell over, and I fell on top. Costa Rica, green coast, environmental conservation, blah, blah, blah, I had had enough. Let's celebrate Bayer and Baygon and whatever poisonous chemicals there are that kill insects and spiders. You can have your ecological diversity and eat it, too.

The treasures of the Costa Rican flora and fauna attract many people from all over the world. There are 160 amphibian species, 200 mammal species, 220 species of reptiles, 850 birds, and 35,000 classified species of insects, with thousands that still remain to be classified. Let's face it; the acre of land that we had bought was nothing more and nothing less than a well-camouflaged oversize anthill.

At this point I needed to get away from everything for a day and I suggested that we visit long-term friends of mine that have a tastefully designed house just a few steps away from the beach near Manzanillo, a village south of Puerto Viejo. As we walked over the wooden planks that bridge the creek to their house, Paul and Vivian met us halfway. The excitement was great. They hadn't seen Miles yet. What a big boy! And how cute! And they hadn't met my husband before. What a handsome young man! Then we admired each other, how we hadn't changed at all! How we still looked so young!

Vivian took us to the local bar at the corner of the street. I was forced to drink a welcome back *guarro*, the cheap Costa Rican firewater. And I was forced to have another two. It was only midday. We decided to quit drinking and left the bar.

Mike, Paul, Vivian and I settled around the barbecue area in-between the house and beach. Miles took off to play with Angel, my friend's granddaughter, at the fishpond. While the kids were catching frogs and releasing them back into the water, I moved my chair close to Vivian's. I was so happy to see her.

'I missed Costa Rica,' I told her. 'It's been quite a while.'

'Well, you know, we always have happy days here. And we are always busy. *Mais* the government is making it *difficile* for foreigners to stay. *Immigración* has already thrown some people out.' Vivian spoke her usual mix of English, French and Spanish.

Then I told her the story that had happened to us the day before.

'A boa. I cannot believe it,' she said. '*Incredíble.*'

'Have you seen many snakes since you've been living here?' I asked her.

'Yes,' she said, as if surprised by my question. 'I have had a boa for a pet. I love boas around the house, and these long green snakes, I forget the name of these things. But it is not *dangereux*. And a boa is not *dangereux*.'

How could she say that after what I just told her, I thought. But then again, she didn't believe me, did she? So I decided to change the subject. I told her about the book I intended to write.

'You and Paul have traveled a lot with your two daughters, right?'

'*Oui, oui.*' She thought for a moment and then she added in her strong French accent, 'All *owar*.'

'And how did they like it?' I continued to ask.

'My older *dautter*, she hated it. Today she lives in *Californie*, and she swear she will never move again in her life.' Vivian laughed.

Maybe that will be Miles one day. Maybe he will hate me for all the traveling we did. Would I be disappointed?

'My younger *dautter*,' Vivian said, 'she totally loved it. She travels a lot with her own *dautter* now. I think it is the right thing to do. It open their minds. We traveled in a Volkswagen bus from the Netherlands down to Morocco, back and forth, and our *dautters* were two and four.'

Wow, I hadn't known that. I was speechless. Vivian got up to prepare a few snacks for us. No, she didn't want any help. Being the excellent cook that she is, she probably thought I would mess up the food.

Paul and Mike were involved in a conversation about constructing houses, which I didn't want to join. So I sat there involved in just my own thoughts. I watched Miles and Angel. They still played with those frogs, which were actually toads. I wished I had been brought up with fewer apprehensions when it comes to bugs 'n' things. The children here don't know these fears. They play with the real creepy and crawly. They don't have plastic daggers and rubber turtles. They play with machetes and pet snakes. And I'd better get used to the idea.

22

Much too Settled

One day I looked at Miles and I knew the time had come to leave Costa Rica, to quit the traveling for a while, to let him go to school and make friends, to let him experience neighborhood and sport clubs, yes, and to bite my tongue and allow him to watch TV. During the last few weeks in Puerto Viejo Miles had visibly grown taller. He had also grown more independent from his Mama and Papa. He made his own choices who to listen to and with whom to spend his time. We were in fierce competition with his new friends Gerardo, José and Nadine, and more often than not we lost.

The little *Tico* guys meant the world to Miles. He often fought with Gerardo. Upset, he would come to me and tell me, Gerardo is so mean, Mama. But under no circumstances was I allowed to say anything bad about him. Instead, two seconds later he would change his mind about Gerardo and ask me if he could go over to him and play again.

After we had worked together on the *finca* in the mornings I wouldn't see much of Miles in the afternoons, unless I took him and his friends to the beach.

On one of those afternoons, the three boys walked in front of me barefooted with their boogie boards under their arms, their tiny swimming trunks on, along Black Beach. Nadine was still too young to go to the beach without her mother. From where we stayed at Black Beach it was about a quarter of a mile into the village of Puerto Viejo, or Old Harbor, as it was called back in the times when the predominant language was Creole English. Where the beach curls around the black sand turns into white sand. We reached town.

When the 1991 earthquake lifted the coral reef along the Southern Caribbean of Costa Rica, it constructed a perfectly round, natural pool in front of Puerto Viejo where it is safe for the village children to swim. Miles and his friends jumped and splashed for hours in the basin that was bubbling with local kids. Many of the kids can't swim which I found surprising since they live by the ocean. On the other hand, swimming doesn't come as natural as you would think to most humans, so unless you are properly instructed you may be able to keep yourself afloat, but you can't swim. I have a hard time myself instructing Miles. He swims with his head underwater and, therefore, he doesn't make it very far.

After an hour of swimming I took the kids to the Chinaman and we bought coconut flavored ice cream. *El Chino*, as the Spanish-speaking people in town call him, has a beachfront store in the wooden building that is the size of one city block. *El Chino* owns the entire building which is constructed in the

Caribbean style on low stilts. But why can't he be bothered to paint his building? It looks a weathered, faded, peeled off green. Maybe he wants to look poor or simply fit in with the majority.

The store is a supermarket, souvenir shop, kiosk and bank, all in one. Everything that is sold here is neatly stacked on the shelves that wrap around the entire room from the bottom to the enormously high ceiling. A member of his family sold me the ice cream for the kids from behind the counter. I sat with the boys on the front porch. We swung our legs, stared at the sea and watched tourists and locals pass by.

On another afternoon, the boys stayed at Gerardo's farm and played with the dogs and puppies. Miles's favorite dog is Lila. She is the ugliest dog of the pack, a sausage dog with a rat's face. But she just had six puppies and, I guess, that's the attraction. We bathed all the dogs and scrubbed them with a special shampoo that kills fleas. Then we got some coconuts and the boys climbed the cashew tree and swung in the hammocks. Gerardo's mom and I cooked dinner, coconut rice, fried plantains and fresh tuna steaks. We dressed in long pants and long-sleeved shirts so that the mosquitoes wouldn't get us. We sprayed some repellent on our ankles, then we sat outside in the *rancho*, an oversize tiki hut and ate.

Two months is sufficient time for a five-year-old to consider a small town like Puerto Viejo his home. When you know all the streets in town, all the restaurants and shops, when people recognize you, greet you, and invite you to their homes, when you don't feel a stranger anymore, then it doesn't matter where you are in the world, the place becomes your home. However, if you happen to have strong roots to a place somewhere else, then these will always override. I never had very strong roots to my country of birth. I have always felt more at home in Costa Rica. Children who have moved around the world as much as Miles feel very quickly at home. It is the place where he, his family and his friends live. Anything else is secondary.

Our daily routines in Puerto Viejo revolved very much around the natural environment. We awoke with the sunshine. We hurried to have breakfast and to get to work before it got too hot to travel along the gravel roads. The birds and animals of the jungle welcomed us with their whistling, whooping, singing and screeching. They silenced as the day got hotter. We checked on the gigantic green iguana in the tree. It hadn't moved. Then we began to sweat in our boots and long pants, but that's what you have to wear when you work in the rainforest, for your protection. All your senses are on alert when you are in the jungle surrounded by trees with straight trunks so tall that they poke a hole in the sky. We made sure that Miles didn't step into a colony of fire ants and that he didn't trip over buttress roots. During lunchtime we sought shelter in the shade. In the afternoon Miles played until darkness commanded an end to any running games in high grass.

Miles doesn't get me angry easily. He is a good kid. Nevertheless, one morning he did get me pretty mad. He woke up, climbed out of bed and ran to the window. He had heard Gerardo's voice. Without acknowledging my awake presence (I had called his name), he opened the *cabina* door and ran outside, still in his pajamas. Although furious I let him go. We had had so much quality time together, so much playing and talking, seeing and enduring, it was okay that he would take off now to be with someone his age who wouldn't tell him what to do. There was no reason for me to react jealously.

After we had pedaled our bikes to our property for a last visit, I walked hand in hand with Miles across the forest floor and we said good-bye to all the amazing things that we had planted: the avocado tree, the breadfruit tree, the lemon and orange trees, the *nispero* tree, the lipstick palm tree, the traveler's palm tree, the Bismarck palm tree, the ginger, the pineapple and the bromeliads. We hid our garden tools behind some trees and showed our gardener where he would find them. José is from Nicaragua. He is a wonderful man, always friendly, hard working and loyal. Nicaraguans are lazy, and before long they rip you off. Nicaraguans are criminals, they say in Costa Rica. But that never bothered us. Every so often José would come on his horse and bring the other two horses that he had when he came to work for us. The day we said farewell he had brought them so Miles could go for a ride with him in the jungle. He had also brought two huge white sacks filled with coconut palms. We planted them together along one side of the property.

'*Vaya con Díos.*' May God be with you, José said, and I knew he meant it. When he gave us hugs, he had tears in his eyes.

'*Nos verémos el año que viene.*' We will see you next year, I said, and hoped that I would be able to keep my promise.

Miles was upset. He didn't want to leave. He had never been upset like that before, not even when we left England, where we had lived for three years, on and off. I tried to divert his attention and told him we would go and visit a huge mountain before we flew home. In this mountain there lived a dragon that would spit fire at night. It sounded exciting enough to at least dry his tears.

Feeling guilty for having condemned my husband to several months in Puerto Viejo instead of touring Costa Rica, I decided that we had to go and see at least one other place besides the Southern Caribbean. I chose the Arenal Volcano and, as a treat, an afternoon in the Tabacón Hot Springs. The resort and spa is built around a chain of natural pools filled with steaming hot water. Surrounded by tropical gardens, you relax in the hot water while you can hear and see the volcano erupt as often as every 25 minutes. Unfortunately, the water was far too hot for Miles. I really hadn't thought this through very well. We made up for it with a delicious steak dinner and then we rented an A-framed *cabina* for the night with mountain view.

It was a cool evening and we huddled up in the woolen blankets that we found in the closets. Then we sat next to each other on the small porch facing the volcano. Miles sat in the middle. He stared into the complete darkness. Bit by bit our eyes got used to the dark and we could make out the lines of the mountain. Suddenly we heard a growling like a thunder in the distance.

'It's the dragon,' Miles shouted excited.

'What did it say?' Mike asked.

Miles shrugged his shoulders. 'I don't know. I couldn't hear it.'

Was he playing a game with us or did he believe in the dragon? All of a sudden glowing red and orange lava shot out of the crater and ran down the mountain, first like glue, then the last bits of lava like snowballs. Miles was amazed.

'The dragon is really spitting fire,' he exclaimed.

The mountain silenced. The lava died. And there was no more. Miles got tired, but Mike and I stayed on the porch just staring into the dark. Our world trip had come to an end and I wanted to say important words about what a great traveling companion, husband and father he had been and how much I loved him. I am the talker of the two of us, the one with more energy once the sun has set. I am the night owl, but that evening, that all-important evening, I fell asleep. I couldn't help it. In the middle of our conversation my eyes closed and I fell to the side. Mike let me sleep. Perhaps he knew how much I needed it.

Suddenly, the volcano erupted again. Mike shook me so I could enjoy the spectacular performance with him. I woke slowly, not really understanding what had happened. Then I leaned my head against his shoulders and it occurred to me that never in my life had I drifted off unintentionally. I am no couch sleeper. I go to bed before I fall asleep. I knew then that in nine months Miles would have a baby brother or sister to travel with.

23
Epilogue
Alaska
A Fresh Beginning in a
Cooler World

Tell me, and I forget.
Show me, and I may not remember. Involve me, and I'll understand.
Native American saying

How far is it from Washington, D.C. to Anchorage, Alaska? I suffered from morning sickness, Miles laid across the backseats with a flu and fever. Mike drove. The scenic route past Canada's lakes and through British Columbia is dull in November, even more so when you feel like throwing up for the most part of the trip. You become oblivious to scenery. But I looked forward to living in Alaska.

Herds of caribou crossed the highway as we approached the Alaskan border. Most non-US citizens think that Alaska is part of Canada. It is certainly too far from Washington, D.C. to be ruled by it. Alaska, the wilderness and the people, have a mind of their own. And that's the attraction.

The drains in our apartment stank or could it be that pregnancy had messed up my senses? The sky was gray and so were Anchorage's streets. I didn't have a work permit, so the highlight of my day would be a hot cup of coffee at the heated bookstore café.

Miles started kindergarten. He had a highly motivated teacher, who during recess, was always the first on top of the climbing frame. The kids in his class were very welcoming. Miles was happy and, when the snow fell in December, he was even happier. He adapted from 90 degree heat to 20 degrees below zero as if he had grown thermal skin overnight. The transition from travel food to American junk food was just as easily accomplished. Aren't kids phenomenal?

They nickname Alaska the Last Frontier. It's a state of many contrasts: complete darkness in the winter, bright nights until midnight in the summer. Hot summer days meet the blue ice of the glaciers. Here, Miles entered formal schooling, but at the weekends there was enough space for him to be wild and to comb the forests with a stick and a dog.

We were settlers again. We bought shelves and the things you put on shelves. We bought wardrobes and the things you fill them with. We knew when to get up the next day, where to go and what to do. Life was predictable. It was imperative that we found outlets for our excess energy other than becoming hung up in the nitty gritty of the settlers' problems.

I was glad that I had shown Miles a different life, a different perspective, different ways to spend the day. Traveling had exposed him to such an abundance of experiences, every day he had to make new choices about his likes and dislikes. And although shy at first, Miles developed into a boy who is very sure of himself, his emotions and his opinions. Traveling, by the very nature of it, had nourished his intrapersonal and interpersonal intelligences. Something that's hard to prove on paper, but I can sense it when I watch Miles.

My praise is entirely dedicated to my son. Traveling with him was never a hassle. How well we will do in the future with a second child, with a different personality, I don't know. It might be worth writing another book. All I know is that Miles has set high standards. And all I hope for is that one day, when he is much older and the puzzle pieces of his life begin to form a coherent picture, he will like what he sees.